Simple & Stylish Woodworking

20 Projects for Your Home

EDITED BY SCOTT FRANCIS

POPULAR WOODWORKING BOOKS

CiNCINNATI, OHIO
popularwoodworking.com

Contents

On the Wall 4

one

Sunburst Wall Clock **5**

two

18th-Century Mahogany Mirror **10**

three

Isaac Youngs' Wall Clock **18**

four

Greene & Greene Frame **27**

For Mantels & Table Tops 30

five

Falling Water Table Lamp **31**

six

Kumiko Lamp **36**

seven

Bright Idea Lamp **45**

eight

Stickley Mantel Clock **48**

nine

Voysey Mantel Clock **56**

ten

Tusk-Tenon Bookrack **65**

Shelving & Storage **71**

eleven

Traditional Hanging Shelves **72**

twelve

Bent Lamination Shelves **77**

thirteen

Corner Shelf **84**

fourteen

Wine Rack **87**

fifteen

Shaker Oval Boxes **92**

sixteen

Silverware Tray **104**

seventeen

Japanese Sliding-lid Box **107**

Gifts & Decor **112**

eighteen

Outdoor Lantern **113**

nineteen

Mirrors **117**

twenty

Heirloom Album **123**

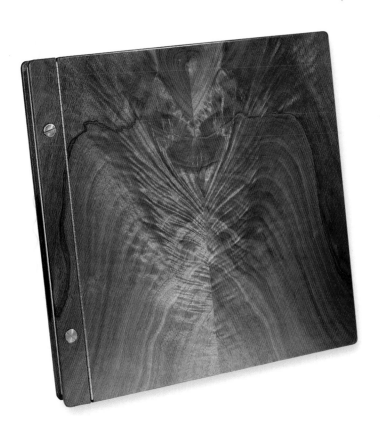

On the Wall

one

Sunburst
Wall Clock

by ANDY BROWNELL

The sunburst-style wall clock came in a variety of shapes and sizes during its heyday of the mid-1940s to the mid '60s. Its aesthetic captured many of the design elements common to the mid-century modern style – curves, colors, acute angles and mixed materials – all elegantly arranged to deliver both beautiful design and function. Designers such as George Nelson with his work for the Howard Miller Clock Company (the iconic polygon clock), as well as his imitators, followed a simple set of three structural elements.

The first is the central structure of the clock face – usually round, and either painted or adorned with a printed metal face of Arabic or Roman numerals, and, of course, the hands of the clock. Next are the spokes, typically round brass rods extending outward in a concentric pattern, and numbering anywhere from as few as four to as many as 48. Then come the rays that connect to the spokes; they often resembled sunflower petals, sun rays, globes or diamonds, and were commonly made from teak, walnut and rosewood.

These three key elements form the basis of just about all of the mid-century modern clocks that were produced last century, and they are replicated today. They also provide the baseline for developing an almost endless number of styles and variations. The version I've built here measures 30" in diameter, has 24 rays and uses Brazilian rosewood and carbon-fiber tubes – an updated look to the traditional brass.

Design at Full Scale

The great part about the sunburst design is that by alternating the number and geometric shapes of the rays, as well as the lengths of the spokes connecting them to the central dial, you can come up with a wide range of variations. My goal was to make two styles of rays efficiently by using the same dimensioned blanks for each style: ½" x 1⁹⁄₁₆" x 8". The inner rays are a straightforward triangle shape, while the outer rays have complex bevels on the triangle sides for added visual interest.

The rays were the perfect place to use some (pre-embargo) Brazilian rosewood I'd been saving for a special project. (Black walnut would also be a good choice.)

To get started, mill the 24 rectangular ray blanks – and make a few extras from scrap wood to use for test cuts. The blanks should be ripped from quartersawn material so you have straight grain on all the rays.

In the period, the rods were typically made from brass – and you can certainly use that for your project. This design, however, uses a far sturdier and lightweight option: ⁵⁄₃₂"-diameter carbon-fiber tubes. To match my design, you'll need 12 pieces at 2¼" long, and 12 pieces at 5½" long. A modified bench hook (bottom left) helps you make consistent cuts. Chamfer the ends of the rods

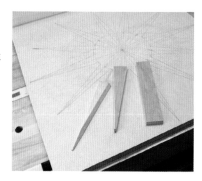

Out of one, many. Working from a scale drawing and common-sized stock materials offers a variety of design options for the final shapes of the rays.

Consistent cuts. A small jig made from MDF holds the tubes in place, and a fine-toothed dozuki saw ensures consistent and square cuts on the tough carbon fiber.

Table saw circles. I cut circles on the table saw using a sled and clamp. The stock is positioned on a small pin centered 3½" from the blade (the circle's radius). Clamp the face, cut a facet, then rotate the piece several degrees for each successive pass to approximate a complete circle.

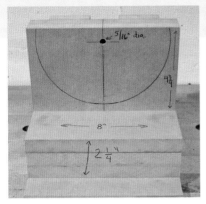

One jig, two uses. One side of the jig (left) holds the face in position at the drill press; the other side (right) holds the ray blanks.

Paper template. Mount a 7"-diameter paper compass printout to the clock dial so you can squarely mark out the location of each of the 24 holes on the outside edge of the face, each spaced at 15° increments.

with #220-grit sandpaper to make them slide more easily in the holes.

For the clock face, I chose Honduran mahogany. Use whatever method and tools you prefer to cut a $1^{9}/16$"-thick x 7"-diameter circle, then drill a $5/16$" hole through the center. Sand the edges fair and smooth with #220 then #320-grit wrapped around a block that matches the radius of the circle.

Precision Matters

Precision is a must with this project, so making many accurate geometric pieces requires some unique but simple jigs. If you stray from this particular design, you'll need to make the appropriate adjustments on the jigs to accommodate your clock's geometry.

The first is the aforementioned jig for the carbon-fiber tubes. The next one (above), serves two purposes on the drill press:

You'll need to affix the clock dial to the jig using a $5/16$"-diameter shaft in the dial's center hole (I used a $5/16$" drill bit) to provide precise vertical and concentric alignment of the 24 rods that connect the dial to the ray pieces.

After you've marked the hole locations, mount the face to the jig, and secure the jig to the drill press to drill 1"-deep x $5/16$"-diameter holes directly in the center of the face's thickness at each of the 24 marks. So that each hole is oriented properly along the face's radius lines, use a square to ensure the $5/16$" center pin is directly in line with the travel of the quill

Now turn the jig around to drill the 1"-deep holes in the ray blanks. Again, take care each hole is exactly centered on the end face and parallel to the blank's centerline.

With the drilling done, complete the clock face by routing a $1/16$" chamfer on the back edge and a $3/8$" chamfer on the front edge.

Precise holes. Moving around the dial, drill all 24 holes with a brad-point bit. Accuracy matters, so be sure to hit as close to the middle of the line as you can.

End runs. Made from MDF scraps, this simple yet sturdy jig helps align the ray blanks to ensure accurate drilling for the carbon-fiber tubes.

You'll also need to inset the clock movement on the face's back. To locate it, cut a scrap piece slightly larger than your movement and drill a centered $5/16$" hole. Use a drill bit to align the location as you orient the movement with the vertical grain of the face. Then remove the waste. (For my movement, a $2^{3}/16$"-square x $3/4$"-deep recess was required, including a bit of wiggle room for easy access for battery changes.)

Now drill the holes in the ray blanks.

To cut the rays to their final shape, you'll need two more jigs; see "The Rays: Precision Geometry" at on page 8. I recommend you first make some practice

All of the rays are designed to end in a blunt point, and use a common set of angles. This is done by two simple sets of modifications to a table saw sled (or simple throw-away versions) using a pair of guide blocks and two cam-lock clamps.

To set up for the interior rays, first cut two guide blocks from ¾" x 7" x 4" stock. On the first block, cut one long edge at a 5° angle, and on the second cut one long edge at 10°.

For the first cut, secure the 5° block to the sled (to the left of the blade slot) such that when a ray blank is secured to it, the near right corner of the blank falls exactly at the intersection of the blade slot and the sled's main fence. (The guide block will meet the sled fence just a bit more than ¹⁹⁄₁₆" from the left of the slot.)

Finally, attach one of the surface clamps to the block to secure blanks for this cut. The 10° block is a bit simpler to position; it needs to be placed such that its rear left corner meets the fence precisely ¹⁹⁄₁₆" from the right edge of the blade slot. Attach the other clamp to the 10° block for the second set of cuts.

This is all much easier to do than describe – but take your time here

because precision and consistency are critical to the final appearance.

Place a test ray blank on the jig tight against the 5° block with the blank's drilled hole facing toward you. Clamp the blank and run the sled through the saw.

For the second cut, flip the test blank lengthwise, and place it to the right of the blade slot. Use the 10° block's clamp fixture to secure the blank and take a pass on the saw. If everything has been set up correctly, the drilled end of the blank should still be full-width at ¹⁹⁄₁₆", with 5° tapers up each edge to the far end, and have a blunt at the end of about ⅛"-³⁄₁₆". Adjust the setup if necessary, and cut the 12 inner rays.

For the outer rays, the jig is essentially the same, but the table saw blade is tilted 30°. Because of the sled thickness, tilting the blade will also shift the blade's slot in the direction of the tilt (by about ⁷⁄₁₆" for a ¾"-thick sled base).

To compensate for this, shift each guide block to the left accordingly. You can either take a pass with the sled first, then use the new slot to reposition the blocks, or make a second sled if you don't wish

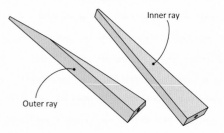

Inner ray

Outer ray

to sacrifice the integrity of the 90° sled. Once the guide blocks have been repositioned, use another test blank to check setup and proceed exactly as with the outer rays.

Sunburst Wall Clock

NO.	ITEM	DIMENSIONS (INCHES)			MATERIAL	COMMENTS
		T	W	L		
24	Ray blanks	½	1⁹⁄₁₆	8	Rosewood	Cut extra for test cuts
1	Clock face	1⁹⁄₁₆	7 dia.		Mahogany	

cuts on inexpensive scrap wood before tackling any expensive stock.

Finishing Up

With all of the pieces cut, plane the edges smooth. A few passes should do it.

Next, move onto #220- and #320-grit sanding. I secured a piece of sandpaper to a sheet of plate glass and "polished" each surface much like a jeweler polishes the facets of a gemstone.

Finally, apply two coats of Watco Teak or Danish oil (avoid getting too much oil in the rod holes), then apply a finishing wax.

Now oil the clock dial (again, try not to get much in the rod holes). Wax all surfaces but the face.

Next, apply some cyanoacrylate (CA) glue to the back of the metal clock face and affix it to the center of the dial, taking care to align the holes at the 3, 6, 9 and 12-o'clock positions. Place a flat weight on top to hold it in place while it dries.

Assembly

Apply a small amount of CA glue in each hole of the 12 inner rays and slide in place the 2¼"-long rods. Repeat this step with the 5¼"-long rods on the outer rays.

Once the glue is dry on the face rods, alternately glue up the inner and outer rays around the circumference. Be sure to make the rays' surface coplanar with the face of the clock; small deviations add up visually.

Finally, attach a picture hook to the back of the clock about ¾" down from the 12-o'clock position and assemble the clock's mechanical movement to the clock dial, following the manufacturer's instructions.

Now it's just a matter of installing a battery, setting the time and hanging your clock in a prominent place to add a little mid-century modern flair to your home.

Vise work. Planing small pieces can be tricky; keep them securely clamped and keep your fingers away from the sharp edges. For the acute-angled outer rays, plane gently as you approach the points.

Not suitable for small children. Assembling this clock reminded me of Tinkertoys – but with deadly sharp points. To make assembly easy, work on a large flat surface that provides plenty of room to rotate your project as you keep the backs of the rays coplanar to the work surface and parallel to each other.

supplies

McMaster-Carr
mcmaster.com or 330-995-5500

Rigid carbon-fiber tubes (6),
.188" OD, 48"
#2153T33, $13.75 ea.

ClockParts.com
clockparts.com or 888-827-2387

6" Ivory clock dial, Roman
#D8211, $7.99

Clock hands set
#HND1081B, $1.20

Mini quartz movement
#MVT7230A, $7.95

Prices correct at time of publication.

two

18th-Century Mahogany Mirror

by JOSHUA KLEIN

A true start. Holding your stock secure, true and square is essential to get the frame to come together right.

E ven before the days of Facebook and selfies, Americans were undeniably conscious of self-image. In both Europe and America, the 18th-century genteel elite kept specialized accessories for maintaining appearance. Among the most important of these was a reflective mirror. Because these "looking glasses" were typically heavily ornamented with elaborate fretwork and gilded carvings, the looking glass itself has become an icon of refinement.

This looking glass is based on a piece sold at Skinner Auctioneers in 2014. What drew me to this example in particular is that it is a vernacular expression of a form often punctuated by excessive ornamentation. It's charming because it reveals the maker's obvious awareness of high-style fashion but intentional artistic restraint.

Traditional Construction

Traditionally, mouldings were stuck in long lengths (8' or more) with moulding planes, then miters were cut along the length to ensure consistency of the profiles at the corners.

As much as we all may appreciate the efficiency of wooden moulding planes, not every woodworker has access to properly tuned ones. But is there another way to cut custom profiles simply, efficiently and inexpensively? There is: Just scratch them.

Using a scratch stock is a straightforward method for making elegant custom moulding profiles without fancy tools. I trace out the profile onto a cutter blank (a piece of an old handsaw blade) with a fine-point Sharpie. Then it takes only a couple minutes of file work to shape the profile (keeping a square edge will help in use). Some folks use slipstones to finish shaping the profile but, because we're using this scratch stock on long grain that is tame, I have not found that extra sharpening step to be necessary.

Because of the consistency of the profile, the primary benefit of scratching moulding is that it is possible to utilize short offcuts for this project.

Start by planing a square edge onto an overlong (and wide) piece of mahogany. It's impossible to get a good-looking profile at the ends; the extra length allows you to fade the profile in and out. The extra width makes it easy to hold the work firmly in a vise.

Draw hatched pencil marks across the surface.

Now, holding the fence of the scratch stock up tight against the stock, slowly begin pushing the cutter away from your body down its length. It helps to tilt

Tilt into it. By leaning the top of the scratch stock forward, the cut magically becomes smooth. If you're bouncing off your tracks, slow down and tilt forward more.

Fading in. It's hard to start the profile on the very edge so I just fade it in. As you progress, the pencil marks will be scraped away.

Four sticks. With the moulding shaped and the four pieces ripped from the board, plane them all to final dimensions.

Stand tall. Instead of attempting to plane the rabbet with the profile down, turn it on its outer edge. It seems counterintuitive but it works like a charm.

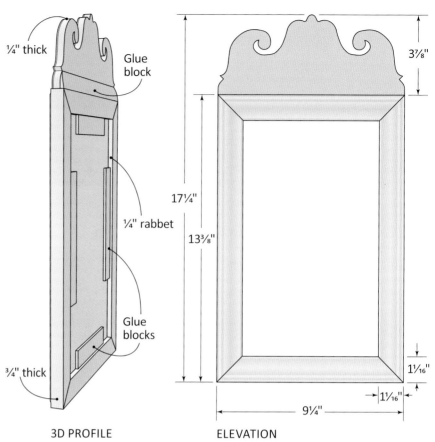

¼" thick

Glue block

¼" rabbet

Glue blocks

¾" thick

Doe's foot

3D PROFILE

3⅞"

17¼"

13⅜"

1 1/16"

1 1/16"

9¼"

ELEVATION

the scratch stock forward because it tends to produce a smoother and more controllable cut that way.

The first passes work better when only moderate downward pressure is applied. Continue scratching until you see the profile begin to emerge through the penciled hatch marks. When the pencil is gone, you're done in that spot.

Short passes are not a problem for the initial scratching; it's for only the last few that you need to make full-length passes with the cutter.

With the moulding scratched (feel free to touch it up with #180-grit sandpaper if needed), use a marking gauge to establish a line for the thickness of the frame pieces and rip the piece free.

Once the pieces are scratched and ripped, place them profile side down and plane them to final thickness. (A toothed planing stop provides excellent workholding for this.)

Rabbets & Miters

The next step is to plane the rabbets in which the mirrored glass will be set.

Planing rabbets on small, short stock like this can be a little tricky. The key is to stand the pieces up on

end so that you have enough clearance to your benchtop for the planing.

Because you will be exerting sideways pressure with the plane's fence, you will also find a notched batten (also known as a "doe's foot") to prevent lateral movement a boon.

With the rabbets cut, turn your attention to the miters. I used my miter box for this, but you could use a shop-made miter box or even cut freehand to lines laid out with a bevel gauge. Because I used my miter box, the accurate miter was easily cleaned freehand with my smoothing plane. This method is easiest if the plane is placed on its side to the bench and the sawn miter is brought to the iron.

Glue the Frame

Forget fancy jigs. You don't even need clamps to glue the frame. All you need is a little hot hide glue. One of the reasons I love hot hide glue is its self-clamping property. In my conservation studio, I routinely exploit this quality when attaching tiny broken fragments that would be near impossible to clamp. I merely hold the pieces in place for a few minutes until the glue gels. As it dries, it pulls the pieces together. The same technique applies here.

Hold tight. With nothing more than finger pressure pushing the joint together, hot hide glue will hold the miter joint tight as it dries.

Check, please. Don't neglect to check for square along the way. It's easier to adjust things while the glue is still tacky.

Extra insurance. Adding splines in the corners of mitered frames is an historic fail-safe in case the glued miter ever lets go.

18th-Century Mahogany Mirror

NO.	ITEM	DIMENSIONS (INCHES)			MATERIAL	COMMENTS
		T	W	L		
2	Top/bottom	¾	1¹⁄₁₆	9¼	Mahogany	Final size*
2	Sides	¾	1¹⁄₁₆	13³⁄₈	Mahogany	Final size*
1	Crest substrate	¼	3⁷⁄₈	9¼	Pine	Final size*
1	Crest veneer	¹⁄₁₆	3⁷⁄₈	9¼	Mahogany	Final size*

*Use overlong & overwide stock; cut the frame pieces to final width & length after sticking moulding

To assemble the frame, glue one corner at a time, working your way around. Apply the hot hide glue to each side of the mitered joint, then press the pieces together. Depending on the ambient temperature, I will hold them with finger pressure for two to five minutes (I use 192-gram-strength glue). Once the first corner is glued, you can move to the next. But move the frame gently – the glue is still drying.

If something goes awry, use warm water and take the frame apart to reglue it. (That's another beauty of hide glue: infinite repairability.)

The next day, saw a kerf into each corner and glue in splines from veneer stock. After that glue is dry, cut the splines close to the surface with a backsaw, then pare them flush with a chisel.

Though the glued miter joint should hold up for a long time, it never hurts to have the splines as backup.

Fretwork

The elegant fretwork on period looking glasses was often constructed of a figured mahogany veneer glued to a secondary wood such as pine. So I followed that practice.

I resawed and planed the pine to thickness, selected my veneer piece, then hammer-veneered the crest veneer to its substrate.

Hammer veneering is based on the same self-clamping property of hot hide glue exploited for the miters. Apply glue to both the substrate and the veneer, then press them together with a veneer hammer. The tool functions just like a squeegee, squeezing out the

Pattern Transfer

Posterboard pattern. I made this poster-board pattern by pulling dimensions off a photograph of the original. Dividers are handy for transferring key dimensions.

There are many fancy ways folks have come up with to enlarge and transfer a pattern. The simplest and most enjoyable way I've found is to search for the proportions with my dividers and transfer them to a piece of posterboard of the final width and height. Historic furniture (yes, even vernacular pieces!) was usually designed using classical proportions. This system may sound intimidating but it's so easy to use because it's nothing more than finding simple whole-number ratios. That's why I say it's enjoyable. Besides, how deep will your understanding of the piece be if you just traced a template someone else (or some copy machine) made for you?

Taking the few minutes to investigate the logic of the design not only informs you of what the artisan envisioned, but it also teaches you to design. This is a case of the "give a man a fish versus teach a man to fish" proverb.

Start hunting for the dimensions by drawing a box around the fretwork in your picture. (It is only necessary to do one-half.) First off, spot the high and low spots as well as any peaks. You will find that these key areas in the design are likely going to be laid out in some whole-number ratio. You will notice the bottom of the inside of the scroll lines up exactly in the center of the box you've drawn around it. Also, the spurs on the side peak exactly one-quarter of the way up from the bottom.

As you define these key points, transfer them to your posterboard template. Pretty soon you will begin

Box it in. Start by cutting a piece of posterboard to the exact width and height of the fretwork. Because the design is symmetrical, you can then fold the paper in half lengthwise. You will only be drawing one half of the design. This way, if your cutting is a little off somewhere, everything is still perfectly symmetrical. Don't waste your time drawing this design twice.

Dividing lines. Drawing in these proportions makes seeing the logic of the design a whole lot easier.

to see the road map for the lines emerge. After you have mapped as many places as you can find, it's just a matter of connecting the dots. With a little practice and an eraser, freehanding the curving lines between points is not difficult, especially if you pencil in grid lines. When all is drawn, carefully cut both sides out together.

Bird's mouth. An L-shaped jig with a notch in the top surface for the saw blade makes it easy to saw out the scrolls of the crest, with plenty of support for the work. Because the bird's mouth is designed to clamp in a vise, it's easy to adjust the height as needed.

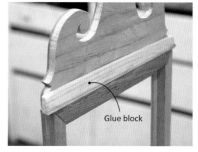

Glue block

Crest support. The crest is not very thick, so adding a glue block on the back is wise. Make sure to taper it on the top and sides so it's inconspicuous.

Beautiful old color. This new old stock veneer has an incredible depth of color not seen on most mahogany available today.

A little at a time. Add your layers of dye a little bit at a time. It's impossible to get a convincing color in one fell swoop.

excess glue while pressing the pieces together. The tack of the glue helps to pull each piece together. After a couple minutes of "squeegeeing," the veneer can be left to dry.

Sometimes the glue pulls so hard it will actually cause the substrate to cup. To counteract this, I place the heart side of the pine toward the veneer. This typically works well, but the use of veneer of period thickness (1⁄16" or thicker) allows for a small amount of planing to regain flatness if needed.

After allowing the veneer to dry overnight, transfer the crest pattern, then cut it out with a coping saw on a bird's-mouth fixture. Cut right on the line. Because there typically was not a lot of clean-up done on period fretwork, leaving saw marks is period-appropriate.

Attaching the crest to the frame is easy: Plane it flat on the bottom and glue it to the frame. I made a triangular glue block to attach to the back for additional support.

200 Years in 20 Minutes

The finish is fun. With a combination of shellac, dyes, pigments and paste wax, 200 years of grime and patina can be convincingly mimicked in no time at all. I think the majority of the finishing time on this project was somewhere around 20 minutes split between two sessions. Because of alcohol's fast evaporation rate, multiple layers can be applied one right after the other.

I loved the beautifully rich color of the crest veneer (it is new old stock), so I shellacked the crest a couple times to use it as a reference for the color of the rest of the piece.

To begin working up the color on the frame and the edges of the fretwork, apply with a rag TransTint dyes mixed in alcohol. In order to give the color an authentic-looking depth, it is important to layer colors on a little at a time.

I ended up using Medium Brown, Reddish Brown, Van Dyke Brown and a touch of Honey Amber, each applied individually in a dilute concentration.

As you apply each layer, you can subtly shift your "brown" to the red side of the spectrum with Reddish Brown or shift it the opposite direction (green) with Van Dyke Brown.

After about 15 to 25 back-to-back layers of color, I gently padded on shellac. This, of course, can lift the color – so don't re-pad an area until it's dry to the touch (only a few minutes). When you are confident that the color is locked in, you can apply more shellac until the pad begins to drag.

At this point, stop and let it dry a bit. After an hour or two, give it a quick scuff-sand with a maroon Scotch-Brite sanding pad to cut some of the dust nibs. Then it's back to padding.

With the finish a little tacky, I dropped burnt umber powdered-earth pigment into the creases of

Muddy it up. By using earth pigments over the shellac, the grain becomes partially obscured. This goes a long way in mimicking years of grime.

The tools of the trade. Just a few simple tools and materials make quick work of matching the frame to the crest.

the moulding. Don't worry about being too persnickety here, because you can always wipe mistakes off with alcohol.

Pad shellac over the pigment to lock it in. By this point you should have lots of layers of colors, pigment in the creases and all the shellac completed. If it looks too monochromatic during the coloring process, you can carefully wipe layers off with alcohol. I almost always do this in the coloring process. It really helps the final look.

After letting it sit overnight, gently level the finish with a maroon Scotch-Brite pad, then wipe down the dust with a cloth and then with your bare palm (it's way better than tack rags).

The next step is, I think, the key. Too often in faux-patinated pieces, low spots and partially filled pores are left with a higher gloss than the surrounding areas. This is the opposite of what we find on truly antique pieces, because the dirt and grime in these places is always duller than the surrounding areas.

To simulate this, brush on a final coat of matte shellac before rubbing out. I use Homestead Finishing's Shellac Flat – an additive that cuts down on the sheen – for this job (homesteadfinishingproducts.com). After an hour, you can safely rub the shellac to sheen. I used "natural" Antiquax paste wax mixed with burnt umber pigment, applied with Liberon #0000 steel wool. The thing I love about Antiquax is that I can buff it to

sheen after only a minute or two. Other waxes I've tried seem to take a lot longer to haze before buffing.

Add Glass & Hang

For the mirror, I used a small piece of salvaged 19th-century material. You can purchase ⅛"-thick glass and have it cut to size from glass suppliers. Or – if you feel up to the task – you can buy a glass-cutting tool from any hardware store to cut your own. It's simple enough to score your line and snap it off.

The glass is held in the rabbets with glue blocks. To hang the mirror, attach picture-frame wire (I wrapped it around slotted screws).

This project is a great introduction to working with hand tools because it's not big or complicated. It could easily be made in a weekend and it makes an elegant handmade gift for a loved one – and it reflects well on your skill.

Matte it down. Using an artist's brush, coat the sanded surface with matte shellac. As the alcohol evaporates, you will see the sheen dull in only a minute or two.

Rub it up. With Liberon steel wool and wax, rub the sheen back up. Excess wax is trapped in the pores, simulating years of grime. A soft, clean cloth buffs it up to a mellow shine.

An authentic look. The sawn edges of the fretwork and the deep, variegated color are the details that make this looking glass appear 200 years old.

Blocked in. Apply a glue block in the rabbet on each of the four sides to hold the glass in place.

three

Isaac Youngs' Wall Clock

by CHRISTOPHER SCHWARZ

It's difficult to open a book about Shaker furniture or to page through a woodworking catalog without coming face to face with a clock similar to this one. It seems that nearly every woodworking magazine and catalog has published plans for a clock with Isaac Newton Youngs' name on it.

So what possessed us to do the same thing?

Well, the goal of this project was to create a version of Youngs' clock that looked very much like the classic original but was built with joinery that a beginner would be comfortable with.

As I began drawing up our plans, I made an interesting discovery. Other plans for this clock that I consulted didn't look exactly like the original 1840 wall clock at the Hancock Shaker Village in Pittsfield, Mass. Many of these other plans made slight alterations to the size of the clock's case or the visual weight of the doors' rails and stiles.

In a few instances, these changes looked good. In others, however, it seemed that the designer – in seeking to make the project easier to build – made the clock a little chunky or squat. So we scanned in a photo of the original clock and scaled the parts using design software.

Suddenly the clock got a little taller, a little skinnier and the top door's stiles became narrower. After we "built" the project with CAD and compared it to the original, we knew we were on the right track.

Of course, we did make changes, but they are mostly invisible to the naked eye. To make the clock easy to build, the case is joined using rabbets and dados. The back piece is plywood, instead of solid wood. And the moulding on the top and bottom is a bead instead of a roundover. All the changes can easily be undone for those seeking Shaker purity.

Finding Rift-sawn Wood

Youngs built his original using mostly rift-sawn butternut. All of the grain in that clock is arrow-straight without any of the arching cathedrals that are common to this somewhat-uncommon wood.

To reproduce that look I sorted through a 4'-high stack of butternut at the lumberyard but came up empty-handed. Rift-sawn butternut, according to the guys at the lumberyard, is hard to come by. So I went with Plan B: rift-sawn red oak, which is plentiful and inexpensive.

Three things are important when choosing wood for this project: Pick boards where the grain is dead straight, the growth rings are close together and the grain is rift-sawn – not flat-sawn or quartersawn. Flat-sawn oak exhibits the cathedrals you see on every red oak kitchen cabinet in every suburban subdivision. Quartersawn oak shows off the medullary rays of the wood as shiny bits of what we call "ray flake." (Ray flake isn't desirable on a Shaker piece.) Rift-sawn oak generally has tight grain lines but no cathedrals or ray flake.

How do you find rift-sawn wood? Some lumberyards sort the wood for you. But if they don't, you can pick out the rift-sawn stuff by looking at the end grain. In rift-sawn wood, the growth rings intersect the face of the board at an angle between 30° and 60°. If the angle

Isaac Youngs' Wall Clock

NO.	ITEM	T	W	L	COMMENTS
Carcase					
2	Sides	¾	3½	31½	
2	Interior top & bottom	¾	3¼	9½	
1	Divider	½	4½*	10½	Notched
1	Back	½	10	31½	
1	Hanger	¾	5	3	
2	Exterior top & bottom	½	5**	11½	
1	Dial	½	9	10¼	
2	Cleats	¾	¾	10¼	
Upper Door					
2	Rails	¾	1¼	9½	½" TBE
2	Stiles	¾	1	11½	Includes ¼" horns
	Glazing moulding	⅜	½	48	
Lower Door					
2	Rails	¾	1¼	9	½" TBE
2	Stiles	¾	1¼	20½	Includes ¼" horns
1	Panel	½	8¾	18⅜	

* Finished size after machining will be 4¼"; ** Finished size after machining will be 4¾"; TBE = tenons both ends

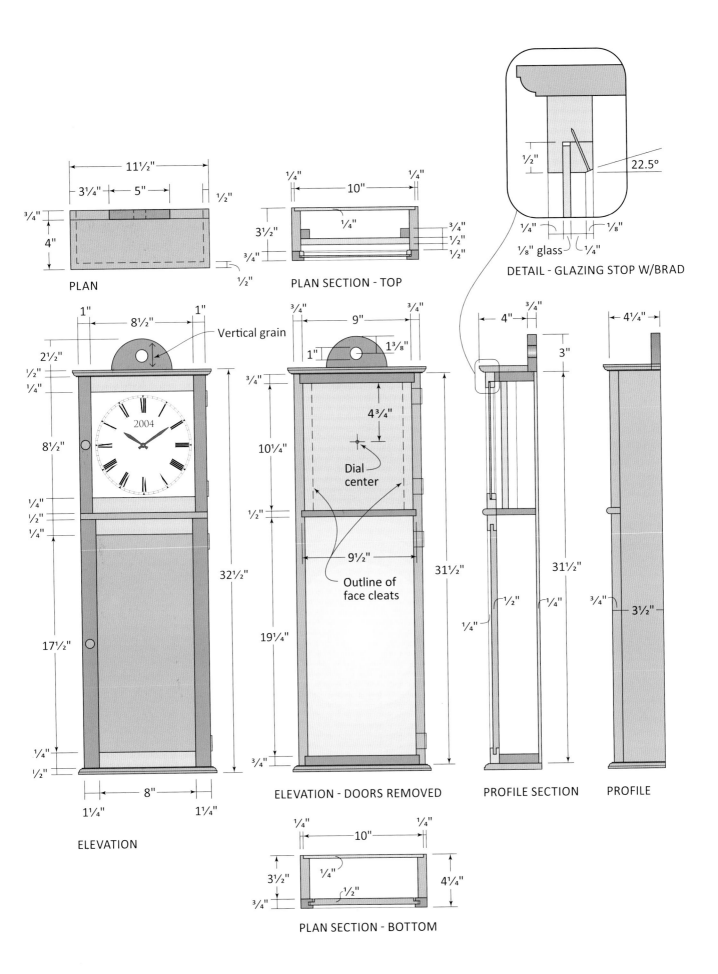

PLAN

PLAN SECTION - TOP

DETAIL - GLAZING STOP W/BRAD

ELEVATION

ELEVATION - DOORS REMOVED

PROFILE SECTION

PROFILE

PLAN SECTION - BOTTOM

Vertical grain

Dial center

Outline of face cleats

With the sacrificial fence in place, this setup will allow you to cut the rabbet in one pass. This eliminates the need for multiple saw setups and you don't need to stand your work on edge to make the cut.

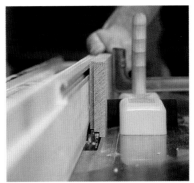

Don't change your saw's setup any more than you have to. By shifting the rip fence ¼", you can make the rabbets that hold the back piece by running the sides on edge.

is less than 30°, the board is flat-sawn. If it's more than 60°, the board is quartersawn. Look over a few boards with this in mind and the difference will be obvious.

I bought 50 board feet of 4/4 red oak for this project. While that's more than I needed, it ensured that I would be able to choose the wood for the rails, stiles and panel with extra care. (If you can't find rift-sawn oak, call Paxton Woodcrafters' Store at 800-325-9800; they can ship it to you via UPS at a fair price.)

As you joint and plane your wood to its final thickness, set aside the straightest, tightest-grained boards for the rails, stiles and panel. Not only will these "look right," they will be more stable and less likely to twist out of shape during machining.

The Clock's Carcase

Here's how the basic skeleton of the clock goes together: The interior top and bottom pieces are secured in shallow rabbets in the side pieces. The ½"-thick divider that separates the doors rests in dados in the side pieces. The back fits in a rabbet cut in the sides. The exterior top and bottom are merely glued to the top and bottom of the assembled case.

It's a bit of a trick to cut notches in the divider so that its front edge runs the entire width of the case. And you'll employ that same trick to notch the exterior top piece around the half-round hanger piece. But it's simple stuff.

Once you've cut the parts for the carcase to the sizes shown in the cutting list, the first step is to cut the ¼"-deep x ¾"-wide rabbets on the ends of both side pieces. I like to perform this operation with a dado stack set in my table saw. As you can see in the photo above, I've added a "sacrificial" wooden fence and a featherboard to my saw's rip fence. This setup allows me to cut right up against the rip fence without leaving a little waste

piece on the end of the board. The featherboard keeps the work pressed to the saw's table.

To make the cut, place a side piece against the miter gauge with the end of the board touching the sacrificial fence. Move the work forward into the cut and keep firm downward pressure on the piece. Check your work with a dial caliper to make sure the height of the blades is correct. When you're satisfied, cut this rabbet on both ends of both side pieces.

To complete the joinery necessary on the side pieces, cut the ¼"-deep x ½"-wide rabbets on the sides that will hold the back. To cut this joint, keep the height of your dado stack the same that you had for your first cut. But shift the rip fence so that you expose only ½" of the dado stack's cutters. Then cut the rabbets on the side with the parts run on edge as shown in the photo above.

Finally, cut the ¼"-deep x ½"-wide dado in the side pieces for the divider. Leave the height of the dado stack alone. In fact, lock the arbor of the saw in place. Then remove the dado stack and put enough chippers and wings on the arbor to make a ½"-wide cut. Also, remove the sacrificial fence from your rip fence.

Clamp a 1"-wide "standoff" block to your table saw's rip fence in the location shown in the photo on page 22. Set your rip fence at the 12" mark – this will put exactly 11" of space between your standoff block and the dado stack. That's right where you want the divider to be. Put a side piece against your miter gauge and against the standoff block. Cut the dado in the side piece and repeat the procedure for the other side. The joinery for your sides is now complete.

Tricky Notches

As you look at the cutting list for this project, you might notice that the divider is longer than the interior top and bottom pieces. It also runs the entire width of the clock's case and stands proud of the doors when they're closed. To make the divider do this, you need to notch the ends so they fit inside the dados and the front rounded-over edge then extends to the edges of the carcase.

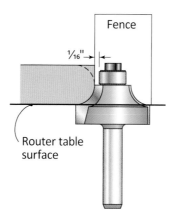

Fence

¹⁄₁₆"

Router table
surface

DIVIDER PROFILE

This is actually easy. Here's the trick: First rout the ¼"-radius roundover on a long edge of the divider, as shown in the drawing above. Next, using your table saw, rip 1" of this detailed edge off of the divider. Crosscut the remaining piece to 9½" long – the same length as the interior top and bottom pieces. Now glue the 1"-wide strip back to the divider.

If you do it this way you will have perfect notches on both ends and the grain will match all the way across the width of the board. (You'll use this same trick to notch the exterior top around the hanger piece.)

Before you assemble the carcase, plane or sand the interior surfaces so they are ready to finish. If you are using sandpaper, sand up to #220-grit. Then perform a dry run without glue to make sure you have the clamps you need and your joints close tightly.

When you're satisfied, spread a thin film of glue in the rabbets and dados and put the interior top, bottom and divider in place. Clamp the second side in place and ensure all the parts of the carcase are flush at front and back.

Compare the diagonal measurements of the clamped-up case to ensure it's square and wait for at least 30 minutes for the glue to dry. Then take the case out of the clamps and secure the joints with nails. (Tip: If you drive the nails in at slightly different angles, you'll wedge the parts together.)

Adding the Top & Bottom

The exterior top and bottom pieces are merely glued to the completed carcase. But before you can do this, you need to do some machining to add the beaded detail on three edges and create a notch in the exterior top piece for the half-round hanger.

Begin by ripping a ¾"-wide strip off the back edge of your exterior top piece. Take this narrow strip and crosscut 3¼" off each end. Now you can tape and glue these pieces back to the exterior top piece to create a notch in the center for the hanger.

Next you can rout the beaded detail on the ends and front edge of the exterior top and bottom. Use the illustration on page 23 to set up your router table. First rout the bead on the ends and use a backup block

A standoff block clamped to the fence as shown allows you to use the rip fence and miter gauge in tandem and reduces the chance of a nasty kickback.

You could wait until the carcase is assembled to glue the detail back in place, but I find that you can get a tighter joint if you do this before the case is glued up. If your joint is smooth, you should be able to use painter's tape to position the detail to the remainder of the divider before clamping.

Using a folding rule – I like the ones where you can extend a 6"-long "finger" from the end – compare the diagonal measurements you make from corner to corner. If they're the same, your case is square. If not, place a clamp across the two corners that produced the longer measurement and apply a small amount of clamping pressure until the two measurements are identical.

behind your work to control tear-out and add stability to this machining operation.

Once the ends are routed, cut the same detail on the front edge of both pieces. Before you attach these pieces, plane or sand the exterior of your carcase so it's ready for finishing.

With that done, you want to fit the exterior top and bottom pieces. These must fit tightly to the case, so it pays to clamp them in place without glue first. Note where any gaps are, then remove material with a block plane from any area that won't ever show to get the pieces to mate tightly. Don't rely on clamping pressure to close up gaps – you should be able to get a tight fit using hand pressure only.

I've found that the best way to attach each piece is to lay it on your bench, then spread a thin film of glue on the mating surface of the carcase and put the carcase in place. Before you clamp the two parts together, secure the pieces with a couple of nails.

Last Carcase Details

Cut the 5"-diameter half-round hanger to shape on your band saw and bore the 1" hole that's 1⅜" from the top edge of the hanger. First glue it in place in the notch in the exterior top piece and secure it with screws through the back of the hanger.

To hold the dial in position, you need to nail in two ¾" x ¾" cleats in the top section of the case. When you position them, be sure to allow for the thickness of the dial (½" in this case), and the length of the stem of your clock's movement. Otherwise, the top door won't close.

Then cut the dial to fit the opening in the top and attach your movement to the rear. When you drill the hole for the stem of the movement, note that it is

When you glue the strips onto the exterior top piece, tape them in place so they don't slide around as you add clamping pressure.

Notch for hanger

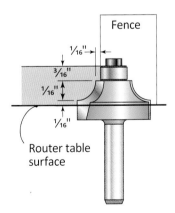

Fence

1⁄16"

3⁄16"

1⁄16"

1⁄16"

Router table surface

TOP, BOTTOM PROFILE

Whenever you can, use your bench to assist your clamping. It helps spread your clamping pressure over a wider area. Here you can see how a couple of well-placed nails keep everything in line as I apply the clamps.

not in the center of the dial board. To center it in the upper door, you need to drill this hole ⁷⁄₁₆" up from the centerpoint of the board.

I used a quartz movement to keep the clock simple and inexpensive. A mechanical movement with a pendulum is another option. If you choose this, be aware you'll have to cut a clearance hole for the pendulum in the divider.

You can find 8" faces at a variety of supply houses or web sites.

Affix the paper face to the dial using a spray adhesive (I use 3M's Super 77 Multipurpose Spray Adhesive) and screw the dial to the cleats using four brass screws. Cut the plywood back to size, prepare it for finishing and screw it to the back of the case.

Building the Doors

Because the stiles and rails of these doors are narrow, there are some useful tricks to machining and assembling them.

The first trick is to cut the rabbets for the top door on wider pieces, then rip the rails and stiles free from these wider boards. This makes cutting the rabbets a much safer operation.

Second, I like to cut all my rails and stiles ¹⁄₁₆" wider than called for in the cutting list. Then I like to cut my stiles ½" longer than the finished size of the door. All this creates a door that is slightly oversized for its opening so that I can then trim the door to be square and perfectly sized after it's glued up. It takes a bit more time, but it saves frustration when doing the final fitting.

Begin by working on the upper door. Set up a dado stack set and sacrificial fence for your table saw much like you did to cut the rabbets for the carcase. Set the height of the blade and the position of your rip fence to make a ½" x ½" cut. After confirming your setup is correct, cut this rabbet on the inside edge of the rails and stiles for the upper door.

Before you switch over to your rip blade to cut the rails and stiles free of their wider boards, it's a good idea to go ahead and cut the rabbet on the ends of the rails. These end rabbets create the lap joint that joins the rails and stiles together for the upper door (see the illustration on page 25). This lap joint, when properly executed, is satisfactory for a small door. To cut this joint on the ends of the rail pieces, leave the saw's rip fence as it is and lower the sawblade so it makes a ¼"-deep cut. Then make the cuts on the ends of the rail boards.

Set these boards aside for a moment and get your rails and panel for your lower door. This saw setup is exactly what you need to cut the stub tenons on the ends of the rails for the lower door and the rabbet on the backside of the panel so it will fit in the door's groove. Cut this joint on both faces of your lower rails. Then cut this rabbet on all four edges of your panel stock.

Finally, install a rip blade in your table saw and rip the rails and stiles of the upper door free to their final width plus ¹⁄₁₆".

To complete the joinery on the lower door, you need to plow a ¼"-wide x ½"-deep groove in the rails and stiles for the panel and for the stub tenons on the rails. Keep the rip blade in your saw and set the fence ¼" away from the blade and set the height to ½". Now plow the groove in two passes. The first pass has one face of the board against the fence; the second pass has the other face against the fence. Cutting the groove in two passes ensures it will be centered on the edge.

Next, prepare all your door parts for finishing. Don't worry about cleaning up the outside edges of the rails and stiles because they'll be trimmed after assembly.

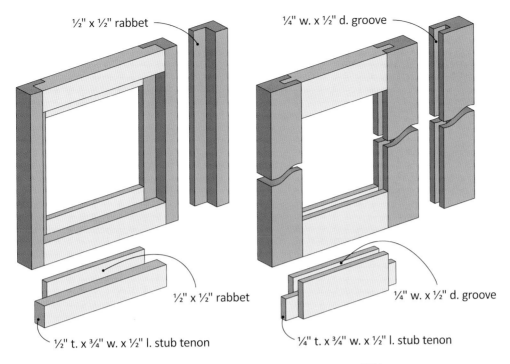

½" x ½" rabbet

¼" w. x ½" d. groove

½" x ½" rabbet

½" t. x ¾" w. x ½" l. stub tenon

¼" w. x ½" d. groove

¼" t. x ¾" w. x ½" l. stub tenon

UPPER DOOR JOINERY

LOWER DOOR JOINERY

Clamping the upper door is a bit trickier than most doors because of the lap joinery. First clamp the stiles against the rails like you would for a traditional door. Don't forget to position the rails to accommodate the ¼"-long horns on the ends and don't use a lot of clamping pressure. Clamp each of the joints with a bar clamp positioned like you would compress a sandwich, as shown on page 24.

The lower door is easier to assemble. Paint glue in the grooves where the stub tenons will go (but not the panel), assemble the parts and clamp things up. Allow the glue to dry and remove the doors from the clamps.

Fitting & Fussing

Now it's time for the detail work. Your goal is to trim the doors so they fit on the carcase with a ¹⁄₁₆"-wide gap between the doors and the carcase. This gap, called the "reveal," must be consistent. If it's not, other woodworkers will quickly notice.

Here's how I trim my doors, though there are many ways to do it: First true one stile on your jointer and rip the door to width, taking equal amounts of material from each stile. Then crosscut the door so it's just a hair longer than necessary. Finally, after installing the hinges, plane the top and bottom of the door to get that perfect ¹⁄₁₆"-wide reveal.

The hinges are a snap to install because they require no mortise. If you lack confidence when installing hardware, here's a simple trick you can use: Screw the hinges

in place on the carcase. Mix up some five-minute epoxy and put a few dabs on the hinge leaf that attaches to the door. Position the door right where you want it, tape it to the carcase with painter's tape and allow the epoxy to set. Open the door and drive in the hinge screws for the door.

After your project is finished, install the ⅛"-thick glass. The most handsome way to do this is with glazing moulding that you machine yourself. This moulding is simply ⅜"-thick x ½"-wide moulding with a chamfer machined on it. Because you'll finish the project before installing the moulding, now is the time to machine and sand it.

Install the Shaker knobs and the catches for the doors (I used a simple hook and screws), then disassemble the project for finishing. Break all the sharp edges with #120-grit sandpaper.

To give the piece an aged look, I chose to finish it with two coats of garnet shellac. Then I followed that up with two coats of a dull-sheen spray lacquer (shellac is very glossy). This finishing process mimics the look of the original clock quite well.

With the project finished, you can install the glass with a bead of silicone in the rabbet, then miter the glazing moulding and secure it with silicone and brads as shown in the construction drawing.

The original clock is hung on a traditional Shaker peg. You could build yourself a "peg board" and array it with a number of Shaker-like accessories. Another

A Closer Look at Isaac Youngs

The Shaker faith arrived in the United States from northern England in the late 18th century. One of the earliest communities existed in New Lebanon, N.Y., and it was there that Isaac Newton Youngs made a name for himself in the early 19th century.

Born in 1793, Youngs joined the Shakers when he was just 14 years old. While the Shakers didn't permit watches (they were deemed "an unnecessary indulgence"), they did value clocks to support punctuality. Many clocks were kept in dining areas and common rooms.

Youngs would grow to become one of the group's chief clockmakers, building more than 20 of these projects over the course of his lifetime. His clocks clearly illustrate the Shaker principles of simplicity, purity and utility. Many follow what has come to be known as the Shaker style – namely, they are straightforward, functional and modest.

Along with his clockwork, Youngs delved into another passion while at the community – music. He helped develop the guidelines of small letteral notation that included material on the importance of melody, rhythm and meter. He knew it was important to teach this system of notation, to provide examples for students to study and to encourage a uniform system for the entire community. Youngs died in 1866.

At its peak in the mid-19th century, there were about 6,000 Shakers living in the United States. But after a long, slow decline in membership throughout the late 19th and 20th centuries, there now exists only one active village, located in Maine.

— Michael A. Rabkin

authentic option is to hang the clock on a single forged iron hook.

No matter how you hang it, whenever you check the time, you'll be reminded that it takes a little perseverance and (yes) time to get any project designed and built so it's just right.

Cringe if you want, but I like quartz movements. They're reliable, require little upkeep and are simple to install. I know this from installing and adjusting several mechanical movements in clocks over the years. Do whatever makes you happy on this point.

When working on narrow stock such as the door rails, it's safer to cut your joinery on a slightly wider board (this one is about 4" wide) and cut the part free when the joinery is complete.

four

Greene & Greene Frame

by ROBERT W. LANG

The Gamble House Centennial

1908–2008

Greene & Greene

t's easy to get caught in the trap of design by formula. But if art were simply a matter of ratios, a paint-by-number Mona Lisa would be just as good as the one hanging in the Louvre Museum. The curves and lifts that exemplify the work of Charles and Henry Greene are a good example of this.

I made this frame for a class to show how to lay out and shape typical details. The term "typical," however, doesn't really apply to Greene & Greene; each house and the furniture within share elements, but subtle differences separate them from one another. Within the style are variations.

First, the Functional Form

In several of the homes designed by the Greenes, items as small as light switches and picture frames were included. Many of the frames have the basic design

Variable curves. The radius of the rounded edges varies along the length of the edges. A series of rasps will allow you to go from rough to nearly ready in a short period of time.

Final slices. A curved-edge card scraper efficiently removes the marks left by the rasp and removes any high spots along the edges.

seen here: The stiles are within the rails, and the thicker rails extend past the stiles.

A mortise-and-tenon joint makes the connection at each corner, and I made the joints first. Because the rails stand proud of the stiles by ⅛", I did the layout from the back edges to keep these faces flush.

I made the mortises with a ¼" chisel in the hollow-chisel mortiser and cut the tenon shoulders by hand. I set up a fence on the band saw to cut the tenon cheeks, and adjusted the fit of the joints with my shoulder plane and a float.

With the unshaped parts dry-fit, I used a router with a rabbeting bit to form the ½"-deep by ⅜"-wide recess for the art. After routing, I squared the corners with a chisel, then marked the locations for the ¼" and ⁵⁄₁₆" square pegs to fall within each joint.

Please Ignore the Pattern

The pattern on the next page gives the basic shapes I used, but I would encourage you to try your hand at developing your own design. Begin by making vertical centerlines on the top and bottom rails, then take several pieces of paper, cardboard or thin plywood and practice drawing.

On the bottom rail, the step is approximately ¾" vertically. Draw a line parallel to the bottom edge, and mark where the edges of the stile meet the rail – this is where the curves begin. The two radii at the end of the rail are roughly quarter circles, but don't use a compass or a template; sketch them by hand until they look good to you.

Connect the line and edge with an extended "S" shape. Sketch this shape as well, without relying on any instruments. If you don't like your first attempt, try again.

The shape at the top is similar, but the stepped line angles down about ¼" toward the outer end. The center portion is a gentle arc, and the two ends aren't vertical; they angle in about ⅛" from bottom to top. When you're happy with the shape, transfer the pattern to the wood.

If you used paper, you can transfer the layout by rubbing the back of the paper with a No. 2 pencil in the general location of the lines. Flip the paper over, tape it to the wood and trace the lines. The graphite on the back of the paper will work like carbon paper.

Over the Edge

The general shape is only half the battle. The edges are all rounded over, but the radii aren't consistent from edge to edge, and they vary along the edges. Before shaping, mark where the stiles land on the rails.

Start with a radius on the long edges of the stiles. Use a block plane or a rasp rather than a router. The inside edge has a small radius with the corner barely knocked off, leaving a flat of wood next to the glass. The outer edge has more of a curve, approximately ¼" at the bottom, tapering smaller to the top.

You can't taper with a router unless you make a jig. You can cut this tapered curve with your block plane in less time than it takes to find the router's wrench. Begin by making a bevel, then keep knocking off the corners until a rounded shape is formed.

A block plane can also be used for the straight edges of the rails. Be careful to stop before the pencil line that's drawn where the face of the stiles meets the edges of the rails.

A rasp will let you handle the more complex edges. The same tactics used with the plane also work here: Make a bevel, then remove the corners until a curve is formed. Remove more material at the ends as seen in the photo, then blend the shapes together.

A card scraper will remove the marks from the rasp. Follow up with some fine sandpaper to blend the flat areas into the curves, and to leave a consistent surface for finishing. I applied a few coats of Danish oil before mounting the glass and artwork. This handwork involves some effort, but the end results are worth it.

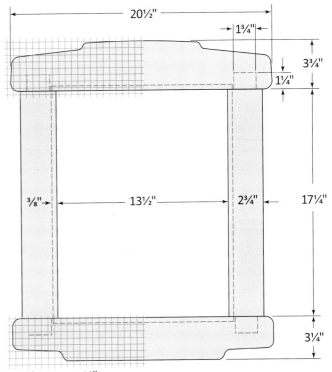

1 grid square = ½"

ELEVATION

Greene & Greene Frame

NO.	ITEM	DIMENSIONS (INCHES)			MATERIAL	COMMENTS
		T	W	L		
2	Stiles	¾	2¾	19¾	Mahogany	1¼" TBE*
1	Top rail	⅞	3¾	20½	Mahogany	
1	Bottom rail	⅞	3¼	20½	Mahogany	

* TBE = tenon both ends

For Mantels
& Table Tops

five

Fallingwater Table Lamp

by DAVID THIEL

Some simple store-bought hardware and some black spray paint turn shop scraps into a dramatic table lamp.

For years I'd been hearing stories about the wonders of Frank Lloyd Wright's house built for the Kaufmann family in western Pennsylvania. Fallingwater was a name mentioned in reverence, so when my travels took me into that area I knew I had to make time to visit and see what the fuss was about. Built in the 1930s and combining International and Usonian architecture, the house was built on top of a waterfall, providing spectacular views for the residents and challenging construction issues for the builders. The house itself has the feel of a space designed for entertaining (as it was), with large common areas and a well-appointed guest house. While impressed with the setting, I walked away from my visit with a different image stuck in my mind: A simple table lamp of walnut with a black metal base that threw a soft, warm, indirect glow against the home's walls.

After examining some pictures, I headed for the drawing board and adapted the concept to a working design that replaced the metal base with a painted maple base. The scale is a bit different from the originals, but the effect and beauty is still the same. I was shocked at how simple the construction was, and I quickly headed for the workshop. After only a few hours I was ready to add a finish and plug in the lamp.

Picking the Walnut

Probably the most important part of this project is selecting the best walnut for the shade. It doesn't take a lot of wood (in fact, you might be able to build this project from your scrap pile), and I resawed the pieces to get a bookmatched shade. If you're a beginning woodworker, this is the trickiest part of the project. First, select a nice piece of ¾"-thick walnut with a figure that you find pleasing. For some, that might include sap streaks or small knot holes. Cut the piece oversized (4" x 21"). Next, set up your band saw with a ½" blade (⅜" will work in a pinch). Check the guide blocks and thrust bearings to make sure they hold the blade tight and don't allow too much side-to-side wandering. If you don't have a rip fence on your band saw, you can make a simple one by screwing two pieces of wood together to form an "L." Make sure the fence is square, about 4" high and long enough to easily clamp to the band saw's table. Clamp the fence to the table ⅜" from the band saw blade. This should cut the piece of walnut evenly

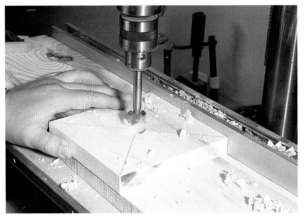
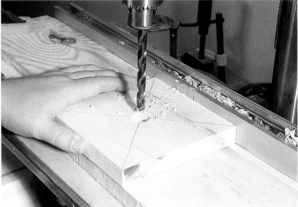

After finding the center of the lower base piece by drawing a line connecting the opposite corners, I set up the drill press to make a 1"-diameter hole, ⅜" deep with a Forstner bit (left). A fence and stop block clamped in place held the block just where I needed it. I then replaced the Forstner bit with a ¹³⁄₃₂" brad point bit (to allow a little clearance for the ⅜" threaded tube) and used the same setting to drill the rest of the way through the center of the block (right). I then reset the fence and stop block and drilled through-holes in the upper base block as well.

down the center and leave plenty of wood to clean up the rough band-sawn edge with a planer.

Start the saw and slowly feed the piece into the blade. Let the blade cut as slow as it wants to. If you force the piece, it's more likely to cause the blade to wander off center and give you two uneven finished pieces.

Once the piece is resawn, head for your planer and run the two halves down to the ¼" thickness. Mark the long edges that will be joined together and head to the saw. Crosscut the two pieces to the 16" length, but hang on to the falloff pieces. One will become the bottom of the shade. With the edges that will be joined against the rip fence, cut the two pieces to just over 3½" wide. Then swing the blade to a 45° bevel and bevel the two center edges. If you're using a good-quality rip blade in your saw and make the cut carefully, you should be able to use the chamfered edge as a glue joint without any further edge preparation.

Cut the shade bottom from one of the ¼" falloff pieces, then set everything aside. Before you can glue the shade together you need to make a hole in the base piece, and it's just as easy to drill all the base pieces at once.

The Drill Press is Your Friend

The base itself is simple. It's two blocks of wood with a chunk of dowel rod glued to the top. The only part demanding care is drilling the hole through the center of the three pieces to hold the lamp hardware. That's where a drill press comes in handy.

After cutting the blocks to size and trimming the ½" off the end of a 1¾"-diameter dowel rod, you need to mark the center of each piece, then drill recesses in both the lower base and shade support and through-holes in all three pieces. Use the photos on page 34 to complete this step.

Once all the pieces are drilled, sand them to #150 grit, then assemble the base. I used the lamp hardware itself (the 3" x ⅛" ID threaded tube, two 1" washers and two ⅛" ID knurled nuts) to align the base pieces and clamp the base together. In addition, to hold the two square pieces properly aligned, I drilled and countersunk two holes in the bottom base, then screwed the two base pieces together.

Use just a little glue to hold the three pieces together, as the lamp hardware will do most of the holding. Plus, you don't want any extra glue squeeze-out to clean up. With the bases assembled, spray paint the bases with flat or semi-gloss black paint.

Finding the center of a disc is harder than you might think. Sure they sell center-finding tools for $5, but I wasn't in a hardware store! After a couple of minutes of thinking, I figured out how to use a try square and the head from my combination square to do the job. Make three pencil lines bisecting the disc to make sure you have an accurate center. Then, using the same bits and methods as on the square base blocks, drill a ³⁄₁₆"-deep recess and a through hole in the 1¾" shade supports. Because of the round shape, the block will spin as you drill, so I used a fall-off piece to apply extra pressure against the block to hold it tight against the fence and stop block.

While the paint is drying, head back to the shade. With the shade base now drilled for the hardware, finish-sand all the shade pieces before gluing. Don't plan on sanding the shade too much after it's assembled because even though it's a fairly sturdy shade you don't want to put too much pressure on it.

With the shade ready to assemble, follow the photos to make the process simple and clamp-free. After the shade is glued-up, sand all the edges to give a softer appearance. Then you're ready to add a clear finish and let the beautiful walnut pop.

Finishing Touches

During the past year or two I've become fond of using lacquer in a spray can for small projects. It's not the least expensive way to put on a finish, but it dries quickly between coats, provides an even and durable finish and requires nothing more than a well-ventilated work area. Two cautions: This method is really only recommended for smaller projects as it becomes difficult to spray on an even finish over larger areas. Also, make sure you're spraying lacquer and not a urethane-based spray finish. Read the label carefully. Even though it may not call the product lacquer, if it recommends 30 minutes or so between coats, you've got the right stuff (and it usually takes less than 30 minutes to sand and recoat).

With your finish applied to both the shade and as a top coat on the base to protect the paint, you're ready to wire the lamp. I've provided information on two types of hardware kits. One offers a simple on/off turn switch on the socket, while the other offers a dimmer switch on the socket. While more expensive, I've found that I enjoy the ability to adjust the intensity of the light emitted to fit my mood.

Neither kit includes the 40- or 60-watt display bulb and light cord, which can be purchased at most any hardware store.

I've got two of these lamps wired together on my fireplace mantel, and another on my desk. This project lends itself to making more than one at a time, so consider where your house can benefit from extra ambience, or think about special friends or relatives who deserve a nice gift.

Whether you're using regular glue, cyanoacrylate or a new fast-drying polyurethane, the easiest way to glue the shade's miter is using masking tape. Align the two halves face-up on a flat surface and push the mitered edges together. Carefully apply a strip of masking tape along the joint, pressing to keep it tight to the wood. When you lift the two halves and fold them at the joint, the tape forces the miter together. Flip the shade over (miter gap up) and add glue to the joint (left). Fold the two halves together, using the shade base as a guide to keep the shade square (right) as the glue sets. Then apply glue to two edges of the shade base and glue it to the inside of the shade, holding it flush to the bottom edge of the shade. The wax paper makes this task easier without gluing the whole thing to the work table.

Fallingwater Table Lamp

NO.	ITEM	DIMENSIONS (INCHES)			MATERIAL
		T	W	L	
2	Shade halves	¼	3½	16	Walnut
1	Shade bottom	¼	3¼	3¼	Walnut
1	Lower base	⅞	6¼	6¼	Maple
1	Upper base	⅝	4¼	4¼	Maple
1	Shade support	½	1¾ dia.		Dowel
1	8' Lamp cord and bulb from your local hardware store				
1	Lamp hardware kit #70266 1-800-999-2226, www.westinghouselighting.com				

six

Kumiko Lamp

by RANEY NELSON

I am not by nature organized or detail-oriented. When I was young, I was the guy with the punk rock blaring and the messed-up clothes; the dog often ate my homework. Even as an adult, attention to detail is not my strong suit.

So it used to puzzle me why, as a craftsman, I'm attracted to detailed, obsessive and small-scale work. You'd think I'd have made a better chainsaw sculptor than infill planemaker.

I now realize my shortcomings are why I gravitate to things that seem out of character – because while I'm making tools and furniture I'm also working on myself. With each project, I improve my patience, my focus and my appreciation for details. And, in the end, making what's difficult is infinitely more satisfying than making what comes easily.

Though I'm still the unkempt guy with the music loud, work like this has made me a better craftsman.

Whether you're looking for spiritual attainment, are interested in taking your hand skills to the next level of precision or need an excuse to use a blowtorch, this Japanese-influenced Andon-style lamp is worth the effort. It combines basic hand and power tools with a few purpose-made jigs – and a lot of attention to detail – to produce a beautiful reminder that patience is the key to wisdom.

Plus, you get to set it on fire. Sweet.

Materials

The lamp is basically a four-sided frame and panel, with an outer structure of flame-charred hardwood and interior panels of softwood lattice.

For the outer structure (the legs), oak, ash and hickory look great with a heavy char, while mahogany and walnut look best with a lighter char to retain chatoyance and color.

For the lattice components, straight-grained softwoods work best. "Kumiko" is the general term for the strips of wood that go into the lattice, as well as for the work itself. Traditionally, Japanese hinoki cypress is the wood of choice for kumiko. In North America, both Alaskan yellow and Port Orford cedars are similar to hinoki, and both finish beautifully. If you can't find these, white pine and basswood also work, though the results are not as crisp.

I made a pair of these lamps, one with oak and pine and the other with mahogany and Alaskan yellow cedar.

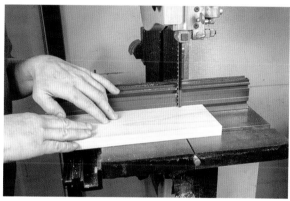

Kumiko stock prep. Start with finish-planed ¾"-thick boards. Joint both edges flat (top left), then finish plane (top right) before band-sawing strips a bit thick (above). This leaves just one surface to finish-plane after the pieces are cut.

Manual planer. The final side of the kumiko is finish-planed as it's thicknessed.

Mitered cheeks. Rip cut at 45° for the tenon cheeks.

Trim the shoulders. A zero-set flush-cut saw rough-cuts the cheeks and removes the waste.

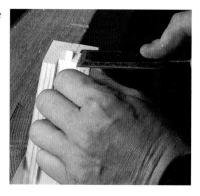

Pare to fit. Then pare the cheeks with a sharp paring chisel.

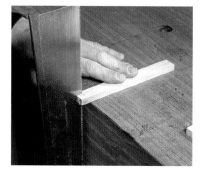

Square cheeks. Rip at 90° for the mortised stile cheeks.

Kumiko Panels

I like to save the fun part (the fire charring) for later, so I start with the kumiko frames. All the kumiko are left unfinished, so the surfaces should be planed clean with a sharp blade. The procedure I use to dimension the stock also leaves the pieces with a beautiful surface and an extremely consistent thickness.

Starting with boards milled and planed to ¾" thick x 8" wide x 14" long, joint both edges square and flat. Then take one or two passes with a sharp plane over the jointed edges to finish this surface before sawing.

At the band saw, rip the panel-frame strips first, sawing ¹⁄₁₆" over the required ⅜" to leave enough material to thickness them later. Set the strips aside and take the board back to the jointer, and repeat the steps until you've got all your frame stock. Now rip the ³⁄₁₆", then the ⅛" kumiko stock using the same procedure.

Thicknessing Jig

For these short lengths of kumiko, a simple handplane fixture does a fine job getting consistent thickness. To make the fixture, rabbet three pairs of interchangeable tracks (⅜", ³⁄₁₆" and ⅛"), then tune them with a shoulder plane for exact consistency.

The tracks are mounted to a dead flat, quartersawn board, plus a few #6 wood screws that serve as stops. Thickness all the ⅜" kumiko strips, then change tracks for the other thicknesses.

The inner frame of the panel, called a "tsukeko," is made from the ⅜" kumiko. I cut the mitered-tenon joinery by hand with my thinnest dozuki, but a good dovetail saw will suffice. (The tenons are ¼" x ⅛" x ⅛".)

For the mortised stiles, I follow the same process shown above but rip cutting at 90°.

Most of the joinery for the inner frame is done using purpose-made mitering jigs (see "Miter Jigs" on the following page). Set the length with the fence piece, and the jig ensures exact consistency on all the pieces.

Lattice

Now on to the ³⁄₁₆" inner latticework. On each frame, there are three horizontal pieces and a single central vertical, all joined by half-lap joints. The two additional vertical dividers are not full-length, and they'll be added once the frames are assembled.

Cut the shoulders for the tenon centered on the end of all pieces. Pop the waste off with a chisel.

Lay out and cut the vertical piece by aligning the already-cut horizontal kumiko with its lower edge.

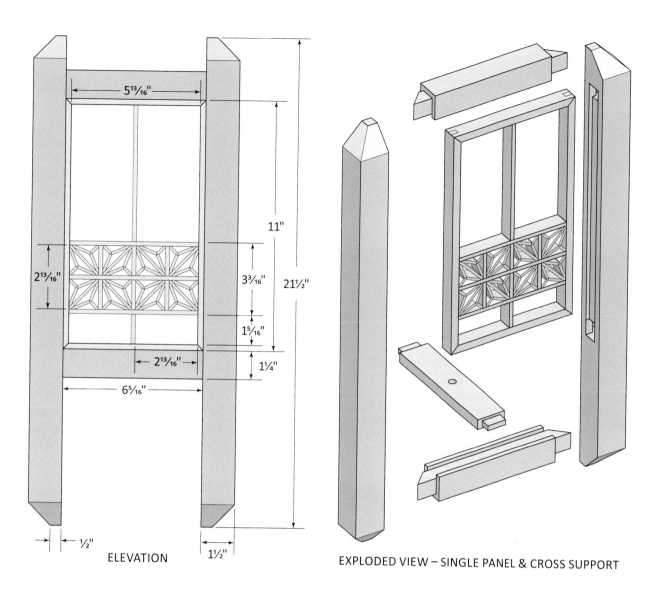

ELEVATION

EXPLODED VIEW – SINGLE PANEL & CROSS SUPPORT

Miter Jigs

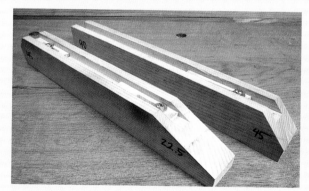

Miter jigs. Nearly all the joinery and cutting of the kumiko happens in these two mitering jigs. Rip a groove about ¾" wide x ½" deep in 8/4 stock. For this piece, 16" jigs will let you use both ends for different angles. You need, at minimum, one 90° end, one 45° end and one 22.5° end.

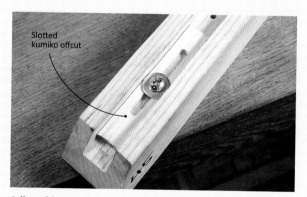

Adjustable stop. Take an offcut from a kumiko and cut a ⁵⁄₁₆" slot in it for use as a stop in the jig. The stop needs to be about 4" long – you can drill several holes to mount it at different parts of the jig for different purposes. You can use pan-head wood screws, but I recommend drilling and tapping for ¼"-20 machine screws instead.

Gang-cut. Mark and cut the central horizontal kumiko carefully; they will be the template for all the other lap joints (as shown below) as well as for the frame's mortises.

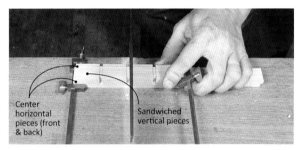

Center horizontal pieces (front & back)

Sandwiched vertical pieces

Half-lap lattice joints. Start with the center horizontal pieces, which have three evenly spaced laps; you'll lay out the vertical laps from this piece to ensure consistency. Layout is simple if you've been precise – set a pair of dividers for 1½" and mark off three lengths from either side.

Ready for assembly. Here you can see the joinery on all the pieces that go together to form the inner structure.

Clamp both ways. While the glue cures, I work on the outer structure.

Next, use a pair of the middle pieces to mark the central half-lap on the remaining eight horizontals. Use the same middle pieces aligned with the bottom of the vertical lattices to mark them off; the spacing from the bottom is identical.

Finally, lay out the mortises in the outer frames using one of the vertical pieces and one of the outer horizontals. The mortises should be just more than ⅛" in depth – the wood in the mortise tends to compress significantly, so be sure to remove enough material that spring-back won't force the pieces out of their mortises.

I don't usually glue the half-lap joints, which are tightly press-fit. I use a dab of glue in each mortise, and I glue the four corners as well. Though the frames are tight fits, I leave them in clamps for several hours to ensure a good bond.

Support Group

The outer frame is straightforward. The four legs are mortised to receive ¾"-square, 1"-long tenons, and both

Stopped grooves. I know of no good way to cut these grooves by hand, or I would. Routers were made for this.

Final shaping. Before lighting them on fire, finish-plane all the outer frame components and put a large chamfer on the long edges. I use a Japanese chamfering plane, which does a spectacular job of making consistent chamfers, but a block plane and some close attention does just as well.

the legs and the rails are grooved to house the kumiko panels. The rail tenons are mitered to prevent meeting. That reduces the glue surface, so pay attention to the fit of the mortises, particularly at the small inner edge.

One pair of bottom stiles gets centered ¼"-thick x 1"-wide x ½"-deep mortises for a cross support that will house the lamp cord and threaded pipe. Cut the lamp support and fit its tenons, then drill dead center for the ⅜" threaded lamp pipe.

For the legs, mark the mortises and grooves for the kumiko frames, and cut the 3⁄16"-deep grooves with a router.

Then drill and chop the mortises, paying close attention to getting the long-grain faces square and smooth. Once done with the joinery, cut the large chamfered faces at the top and bottom of each leg. Pay close attention to the orientation of the pieces – only the outer faces of the leg are chamfered – and leave about ½" of flat area at both top and bottom.

Light 'em Up

The charred finish on the lantern's outer skeleton is done with a propane or MAPP torch. It's a lot like airbrushing, but with much hotter (and cooler) pig-

Chop Micro-Mortises

Burnt is the new black. I use a MAPP torch, held dead perpendicular to the surface, about 4"-5" away to char the wood. Once the color develops, while each piece is still warm, rub with burlap or a Scotch-Brite pad and paste wax to even out the color.

Tiny holes. Cutting such small mortises requires more finesse than most mortising. A single sharp blow with a ¼" chisel defines the longer edges and severs the end-grain fibers.

Hide the evidence. Use a ⅛" chisel to pop waste from top and bottom, so that any compression marks will be hidden by the kumiko shoulders when installed.

Charred. Diffuse-porous mahogany (left) keeps some of its color and chatoyance, thanks to a film coat of shellac. Ring-porous woods such as oak (right) develop great texture as earlywood burns off.

The perfect pop. Waste should pop out like a little spiritual biscuit.

And insert. Check your fit and repeat the initial steps as necessary. With practice, I can get to sufficient depth with a single "pass" of my chisels.

Taking shape. First install the short vertical dividers.

Diagonals in place. Next, cut and install the diagonal inset pieces.

See & saw. A utility lamp, shining into the work at bench level, makes it possible to gauge by eye the depth at which to stop sawing.

ment. Once the pieces are cool enough to touch, buff the wax with a lint-free cloth or finish with a few coats of padded shellac to enhance the depth.

Fill in the Blanks

By now the inner frames should be ready for the insert work. First, cut and install the two remaining ³⁄₁₆" vertical kumiko in each panel. These should be cut to a length of 2¹³⁄₁₆", with a single, centered half-lap joint in each. This can be marked off with dividers just as the lattices were.

Some words about fitting: Even if you've been painstaking, there will be small variations in length of the pieces, so the miter shooting jigs you made for the tsukeko will be in constant use.

The best approach when fitting a set of pieces is to fit to the largest gap first, then systematically shorten the setting of the jig's fence with hammer taps to fit each joint in order of size.

In this way, when you shoot a piece that is too large for any of the remaining openings, those few hammer taps will adjust the jig's fence length and allow you to re-shoot it for a perfect fit in the next-largest slot. Continue this process until you've finished all the installations.

Diagonal Fret Work

After installing the small vertical dividers, fit in the diagonals for each panel. Set the 45° jig fence to 1⅞" (just a bit larger than necessary). It's important to shoot both faces of one end before flipping the piece end for end, or the length will not work out correctly. Check the fit. Hopefully it's just a bit too large for all the openings, so tap the fence on the jig and re-shoot one end.

Continue until you have the piece fit to the largest opening, then shoot another piece to the same size and check its fit in all the remaining slots. If it fits any of them – great. Shoot another piece. Once a piece is too large for all the remaining openings, tap the fence closed a few thou and continue the process.

A Dash of Magic

While you might not realize it from looking at the opening photo, the outside-angled pieces of each quartered section are "hinged" – that is, the wood isn't cut all the way through where it bends.

Sizing the "hinged" pieces is trial and error, but the same length as the diagonal in the last step is a good place to start. Cut and shoot a 1⅞" kumiko strip as with the diagonals, but this time use the 22.5° shooting jig for an included angle on each end of 45°. Use a marking gauge to mark a crosscut line at dead center for sawing.

You're going to saw this piece almost all the way through, but stop just a few thousandths of an inch short to leave a hinge that allows the piece to be folded for installation. This sounds impossible, but it's actually not hard if you work smart. The simplest and best solution is to use a sharp raking light that will let you see how close the saw teeth are to the bottom.

A dab of water on the bottom of the piece will help the hinge pop open cleanly; it should fold with nearly no force and remain intact. Install the piece in one of the panels and check its size. When pressed firmly into the corners, each leg of the hinge should just about bisect the corners. If it is too long, start over with a slightly shorter hinge piece. A bad fit will look sloppy, so try to get a good length worked out. Cut all the hinge pieces to the same length and install them in the panels.

The Keys

And now for the final pieces: the keys that lock the hinges and make the pattern complete. Each key is quite small, and you'll have to do the same sort of large-to-small sizing as you did for the diagonals.

Start by crosscutting all the keys from ⅛" stock at ⅝", which should be oversized. Shoot both faces of one end on the 22.5° jig. Then shoot the opposite end on the 45° jig and check the fit, resetting the fence and re-shooting as required. The piece should just slide in place with light force, locking the entire pattern solidly in place. If there is any wiggle, the key is too small. Don't force a piece, though, because this will distort (or break) the lattice. Again, work from largest opening to the smallest.

Shoji Paper

The last step before assembly is to install paper on the inside of each panel. Traditionally, this was done with rice glue, but I find modern shoji tape simpler to install and repair. Put the tape around the perimeter of the tsukeko frame and remove the backing. With your shoji paper flat and face up on the bench, put the frame on the paper and press gently to adhere the paper. Trim the edges to the frame with an X-Acto blade.

To get the paper drum-taut, spritz it lightly from the rear with water. This will make the paper sag slightly, but once it dries (20 minutes) it will be tight and seamless.

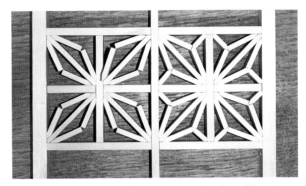

Folded wood. The "magic" hinges are a result of careful and controlled sawing.

Keyed up. Lock everything in place with the keys and take a deep breath.

Stick 'em up. Double-sided tape beats traditional rice glue on all counts.

Wrap it Up & Turn it On

The glue-up is best done in two stages. Glue the front and rear sections first, then install the lighting hardware in the cross support. I used a lamp kit from my local big box store. I recommend an inline cord switch over a socket-mounted one to keep from having to reach in to turn the switch.

Once the front and rear panels are dry, install the remaining panels and stiles, and do the final glue-up. After the glue dries, power up your new lamp and enjoy some good punk rock (loud, of course) and a beverage while you bask in the glow.

Kumiko Lamp

NO.	ITEM	DIMENSIONS (INCHES)			MATERIAL	COMMENTS
		T	W	L		
Outer Frame						
4	Legs	1½	1½	21½	Mahogany	
8	Rails	1¼	1¼	8⁵⁄₁₆	Mahogany	1" TBE*
1	Cross support	½	1½	7⁹⁄₁₆	Mahogany	½" TBE*
Kumiko Panels, Outer Frames						
8	Rails	⅜	¾	6⁹⁄₁₆	Yellow cedar	
8	Stiles	⅜	¾	11¼	Yellow cedar	
Kumiko Panels, Grid						
4	Long verticals	³⁄₁₆	¾	10¾	Yellow cedar	⅛" TBE*
8	Short verticals	³⁄₁₆	¾	2¹³⁄₁₆	Yellow cedar	
12	Horizontals	³⁄₁₆	¾	6¹⁄₁₆	Yellow cedar	⅛" TBE*
Kumiko Panels, Inserts						
32	Diagonals	⅛	¾	1⅞	Yellow cedar	
64	Hinged pieces	⅛	¾	1¹³⁄₁₆	Yellow cedar	
64	Keys	⅛	¾	⅝	Yellow cedar	

*TBE = Tenon both ends

supplies

eShoji.com
eshoji.com or 262-644-7138

Professional shoji paper
#B444, $24.99

Double-sided shoji tape
#Y1B, $2.99

Westinghouse
westinghouselighting.com

Make-A-Lamp Kit
#70266, call for pricing

Prices correct at time of publication.

Bright Idea Lamp

seven

by CHRISTOPHER SCHWARZ

For me, one of the most perfect shapes ever designed is the general-purpose incandescent light bulb. While some people use the word "mushroom" to describe its profile, I've never seen a fungus with such sinuous and perfect curves.

The most elemental light bulb combines a sphere with a perfect ogee. While I'm sure there is some proportioning system embedded in its form, I have yet to decipher it. I just know that if you try to draw it and it's even a little wrong, it looks a lot wrong.

With the advent of the new compact fluorescent light bulbs, the classic incandescent bulb is an endangered species. So to preserve the form of the familiar old-school bulb in my house, I decided to make a desk lamp in its image.

This project requires only a little Baltic birch plywood. The lamp's base is simply laminated discs of ¾"-thick plywood. The curvy shape of the bulb is created by eight identical "blades" of ½"-thick plywood. The only real "joinery" in this project is the eight slots in the base that hold the blades.

Begin With the Blades

The best way to make the blades is to create a pattern in ¾"-thick scrap material. Draw the shape of the blade using the illustrations as a guide. Saw and sand the pattern to perfection.

Cut out the eight blanks from ½" Baltic birch plywood and trace the shape of the blade on each blank. Now nail your pattern to a large piece of scrap that you can secure on your workbench.

Rough out the shape of the blade on your band saw, then affix the blank to your pattern. You can use double-sided tape or even temporarily nail the blank to the pattern. Then use a router with a pattern bit to shape the eight blades.

Bright Idea Lamp

NO.	ITEM	DIMENSIONS (INCHES)		
		T	W	L
8	Blades	½	5	15
5	Large disc	¾	4⁹⁄₁₆ dia.	
1	Medium disc	¾	3½ dia.	
1	Small disc	¾	2½ dia.	

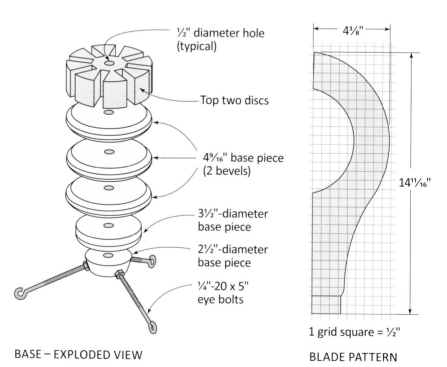

½" diameter hole (typical)

Top two discs

4⁹⁄₁₆" base piece (2 bevels)

3½"-diameter base piece

2½"-diameter base piece

¼"-20 x 5" eye bolts

4³⁄₈"

14¹¹⁄₁₆"

1 grid square = ½"

BASE – EXPLODED VIEW

BLADE PATTERN

Top two discs

Eight notches. If the center of your blank and the centerline of the dado stack line up, then all your notches will be easy to cut. All you have to do is confirm that your layout lines on your blank are vertical before cutting each notch.

Holes for hardware. The edge is angled at 22.5°. Cut that angle on a piece of scrap and hold your small disc against it. Line up your layout line with a line on your scrap or (in this case) a lamination line in the plywood.

The Big Discs

The base of the lamp is a stack of seven layers of ¾"-thick Baltic birch plywood. The top five layers are all discs that are 4⁹⁄₁₆" in diameter. Let's begin with these five.

The top two discs of the base hold the blades of the lamp. Begin by taking two pieces of ¾"-thick Baltic birch and face-glue them together into a 1½"-thick chunk. Square up this piece and mark out the lines for the eight slots: two lines at 90° to one another, and two more lines at 45°. All the lines intersect at one point.

When the glue is dry, scribe a 4⁹⁄₁₆"-diameter circle on one face from the centerpoint. Cut out the circle on the band saw. Sand away the sawblade marks.

Cutting the eight slots is easy with a stack dado set in your table saw and your miter gauge.

First arrange your stack dado's chippers and shims to cut a slot that is the thickness of your lamp's eight blades. Then raise the stack dado to 1⅜". Now screw a tall sacrificial fence to your saw's miter gauge. Screw the blank to this sacrificial fence so the centerline of the slot lines up with the centerline of the dado stack.

Rotate the blank until the line is perfectly vertical. Then push the blank into the spinning stack dado. Rotate the blank. Confirm the next line is vertical. Cut the next slot. Repeat until you have cut all eight slots. Remove the blank and turn your attention to the other three discs that are 4⁹⁄₁₆" in diameter.

These three discs are supposed to look like the part of the bulb that screws into the light socket. Saw and sand each disc to round. Then use a router to cut a ¼" x ¼" chamfer on the top and bottom edges.

The Smaller Discs

The two smaller discs (3½" and 2½" in diameter) are cut round in the same manner as above. On the 3½"-diameter disc, cut a ¼" roundover on one edge using your router. On the smaller disc, bevel the edge to 22.5°. The easy way to do this is on a disc sander with a tilting table.

If you are going to use a metal base made from ¼" x 5" eye bolts like I did, use the photo at right to see how to drill the three holes for your hardware.

With all the discs cut and shaped, drill a ½"-diameter hole in the center of each for the wiring. Now glue up the discs into something that looks like the base of a light bulb. You can do this process one layer at a time or all at once. Your choice.

We Interrupt this Program

Before assembling the lamp, sand and finish all the parts. Mask off the areas that will be glued; stuff packing peanuts into the slots in the base of the light bulb to protect those surfaces for gluing.

Glue in seven of the blades and make sure the eighth fits in its notch with a friction fit – you'll remove that blade to change the bulb when it burns out.

The Metal Bits

To create the electrical part of this project, I used parts from a lamp-building kit from the home center. The 1/8-IP threaded metal nipple is secured to the lamp base using jam nuts. An electric cord snakes through the nipple up to a light fixture screwed to the nipple. (Follow the lamp kit's instructions for wiring, or call an electrician to help you.)

About the Base

I made the base of this lamp using ¼" x 5" eye bolts, though I had other aspirations at the outset. I wanted to use shielded metal electrical conduit to create a somewhat pose-able base – like a light bulb crossed with a spider. Or perhaps even hang it as a chandelier.

eight

Stickley
Mantel Clock

by GLEN D. HUEY

A few years prior to his brothers taking over the furniture business, Gustav Stickley, the grandfather of the Arts & Crafts movement, produced what might at first glance appear to be an ordinary mantel clock. A closer look reveals many remarkable details. It's the details that make this project more than just a box containing a clock movement.

Take a look at where the top of the clock meets the sides. Is Stickley over the top with the number of pins and tails? I guess. But that's a detail that influences the overall look of the clock. Through-tenons that have chamfered ends is another small detail, as is the leaded-glass window that reveals the swinging pendulum. And the 12-sided clock-face opening certainly grabs your attention; it's certainly not as easy to cut as a simple circle. But at the end of the project, you'll have a clock worthy of a sacred spot on your mantel.

Plan Your Dovetails

To be faithful to the original (an example of which recently appraised for $4,000), I set out to cut a total of 13 pins and tails. I wasn't so lucky. In fact, I had to abandon my 12°-dovetail marking gauge in favor of a 1:8 dovetail ratio. Even then, I only managed to arrive at five tails, four pins and two half-pins. The idea is to leave enough width in the pins to hide the groove for the backboard.

After you've established the baseline of your dovetails, layout begins on the top's face with two ¼" sections that become the half pins, one on each edge of the piece. Squeezed between those smaller sections are nine ½" spaces. These wider spaces become the full pins and tails.

Place marks on the face to form the sections. This makes the dovetail layout easier. Use a dovetail saddle marker, or a 1:8 layout jig, to transfer the layout and create the appropriate angled line – each line receives an opposing angled line. Designate the waste area with scribbled lines to ensure accuracy as you work, then repeat similar steps for the other end to complete the pin layout of the top.

Band Saw is Better

I generally cut my dovetails with a 12° angle. That measurement prevents me from using a band saw for the majority of my work without a jig; on most band saws it's not possible to get a 12° setting left of zero. If you use a 1:8 ratio, or 7° angle, that option is back in play so the band saw is my tool of choice.

Measure and mark. Layout on the dovetails begins with accurate sizing. Work from the face to the angled lines on the board's end.

Handsaw-free pins. Pin cuts are easy if you use a band saw set at an angle to match your layout lines. Tilt the table once for each pin direction.

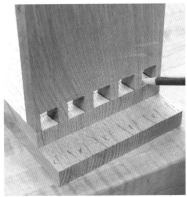

Sharp lines, tight fit. Align the top onto the clock sides, use a sharp pencil to transfer the lines and mark the waste area to be removed. The extra marks assure that you'll waste the correct area.

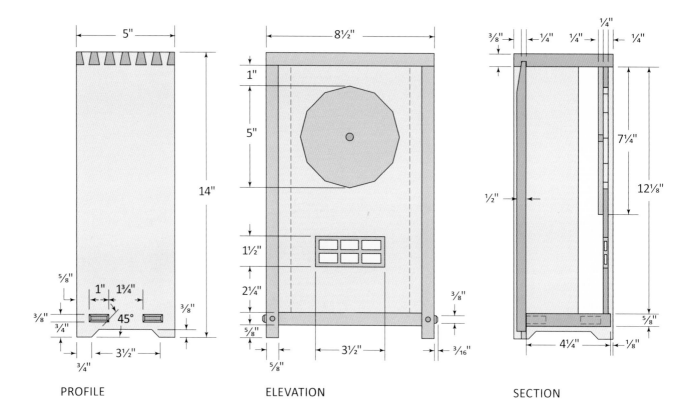

PROFILE

ELEVATION

SECTION

Set the band saw table to 7° or align the saw blade with the layout mark as shown on page 49. The first setting is easily attained with a simple tilt of the table. Make your cuts on the waste side of the lines. (Take a look at the layout in order to figure which line the angle is set for.) Once that's determined, cut every other line to your baseline. Remember to cut both ends of the top piece with the saw's table positioned at this setting.

Next you have to change the tilt of the band saw table. This time the table must be tilted toward the post of the saw. Set the angle of the table, then make the remaining cuts to delineate the pins and tail sockets. Remove the waste area to form your pins.

Transfer the pin layout to the tailboard then remove the waste of the tailboard to form the tails. Set the band saw table back to 90°, then make the cuts along the layout lines on the waste side of the lines. Remove the waste and check the fit. Make any adjustments to achieve a snug, but not a tight, fit. The rule of thumb is: The more dovetails you have and the more dense the wood, the closer to your layout lines you can cut and still achieve a nicely fitted joint.

Easy Mortise for Through-tenons

Once the dovetails are complete and fit, determine the position of the mortises for the through-tenons of the clock bottom. The bottom is ⅝" thick, but the tenons are ⅜" in thickness. There are a number of methods you can use to create the mortises. You can cut them by hand, use a router and jig or use a dedicated mortise machine with a ⅜" mortise chisel and bit installed (that's the easiest way I've found).

Due to the position of the mortises, you'll need to cut the stock moving front to back, instead of side to side as is normal. Place a scrap piece beneath the side to reduce any blowout as the chisel plunges through the workpiece. Locate the mortise area under the chisel. Align the bit with both sides of the layout and position the fence so the front edge of the chisel is in line with the near edge of the rear mortise. Place a stop-block at the bottom end of the side that's 90° to the fence. You'll also need two spacers, one ⅝" thick and one ¼" thick.

Place the side against the fence and the stop-block, then plunge the first hole. Next, slide a ⅝" spacer between the fence and the workpiece. This positions the chisel to cut the opposite end of the rear mortise.

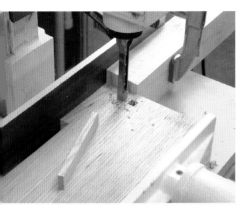

Spacers make quick work. Once the mortise chisels are positioned to the workpiece, it's a matter of changing spacers to complete the mortises.

Watch that cut. Don't push your groove through the dovetail or it will show from the top.

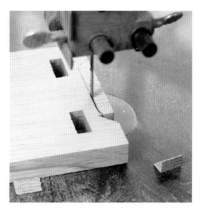

Stand tall. Simple feet are cut at the bottom edge of the sides. The best tool is a band saw.

Accuracy counts. Mark the tenons on your bottom off the mortises cut into the sides. Be sure to accurately transfer the layout once the edges of the pieces are aligned.

Simple and straight. Tenons made at the table will be straight, which makes for a tight fitting mortise and tenon.

Hybrid woodworking. This sander's table adjusts to 45°. Another way to chamfer the tenon edges is with a miter gauge at a disc sander. No matter which method you use, the ends of the tenons require handwork.

Plunge that hole. Replace the thick spacer with a ¼" spacer, which removes the balance of the waste material from that mortise.

To cut the second mortise in the same side, simply flip the workpiece and repeat the same steps. It's best to change the scrap with each new mortise to keep the exiting face crisp. Complete all four mortises, two per side.

The sides are then grooved to accept the clock's back. A ¼" groove is carefully positioned to fit to the dovetail layout. As you can see in the top center photo on the next page, the ¼"-deep groove is aligned with the rear dovetail socket in the clock top and cut with a spiral upcut router bit at a router table. Groove the top from side to side, but for the sides, a stopped groove terminates before exiting the dovetail.

To complete the milling of the sides, form the feet of the clock using your band saw.

Tenons Complete the Joint

After the tenons are created, the piece is reduced in width at the front and back edges. It's easier to locate and form the tenons with the workpiece the same width as the top and sides.

Begin by forming a full-width tenon on each end of the bottom. I use a two-step approach at my table saw. Make the shoulder cuts with the workpiece flat on the table, then with the workpiece vertical, make the cheek cuts to form the tenons. Look for a snug fit.

Position the clock's bottom (with the ⅜" tenons formed and fit to the mortises) onto the clock's sides, then transfer the layout lines to the tenons. Take care to accurately transfer these marks. The tenons should be snug on all sides when fit to the mortises.

Use a table saw to define the tenons. Match the saw blade height to that of the formed tenons. Use a tall auxiliary fence and clamp the bottom in position

Hour by hour. To remove the waste inside the dial cutout, make cuts from the center out, then trim closely to the 12-sided opening.

Raspy detail. Small variations in the faceted edges are magnified when viewed as a whole. Spend some time to bring the edges to your layout lines.

to cut the tenons at your layout lines. Be sure to work on the waste side of the tenons.

Remove the end waste areas using a band saw or nibble the material away at your table saw. The center section can be cut and/or nibbled, but I find it more efficient to use a chisel to remove the waste. Work partway through the material, then flip the stock and remove the remaining waste. Work with your chisel at a slight angle so you undercut the area. Any material extending beyond the shoulder of the tenon will cause problems when fitting the pieces.

These tenons extend through the clock sides by ³⁄₁₆" and are chamfered on all four edges, with a portion at the center remaining flat. You can use an edge sander or disc sander to chamfer the long portion of each tenon, but the work on the ends of the tenons has to be completed by hand with a rasp due to the fact that you'll nip the corner before you reach the tenon's edge.

Once the tenon work is complete and the fit is accurate, make the cuts to reduce the width of the bottom. The front edge is trimmed ⅛" to create an offset at the front of the clock. (Arts & Crafts designers were always looking for shadow lines.) The back edge of the

bottom is trimmed ⅝" to allow the clock back to slide past the bottom when slid into the grooves.

The Focus of the Clock

There's no way around the fact that the door of this project is the focal point. The faceted cutout for the dial is a real eye-popper while the art glass is no small feature. The point here is to find and use a very nice piece of lumber for your door.

Assemble the clock – without glue – to get the height and width of your door, then mill the piece to ⅜" thick. Affix a paper pattern of the dial cutout to the door front with spray adhesive to begin the work. (The pattern is available as a free download at popular-woodworking. com/dec08.) Find your largest-diameter drill bit, chuck it into a drill press and hog out as much of the center of the cutout area as you can, without cutting beyond the facets. The hole size needs to be at least large enough for a jigsaw blade to pass through and the more you remove, the easier the jigsaw work.

Secure the door in a vise or at your bench, then use a jigsaw to cut from the center hole to each facet junction. Next, cut close to each facet line without touching the

Stickley Mantel Clock

NO.	ITEM	DIMENSIONS (INCHES)			MATERIAL	COMMENTS
		T	W	L		
1	Top	⅝	5	8½	QSWO	
2	Sides	⅝	5	14	QSWO	
1	Bottom	⅝	5*	8⅞	QSWO	¹³⁄₁₆" tenon both ends
1	Door	⅜	7¼	12⅛	QSWO	
2	Supports	⅝	1¼	12⅛	QSWO	Rabbeted for dial back
1	Back	½	7⅝	13¼	QSWO	
1	Dial back	¼	7¼	7¼	Plywood	

QSWO = quartersawn white oak; *Oversized, will be cut to fit line. As you reach each center-to-facet junction line, the waste falls away, allowing you to line up the next length of cut. A good jigsaw blade is a must.

Now use a rasp to straighten your cuts. Work tightly and accurately to the lines. If you're off even a small amount, the symmetry of the design will visually intensify any inconsistencies.

Next, lay out the opening for the art glass and again use a jigsaw to hog out the majority of the waste. Fine-tune the opening with your rasp. When these two areas are cut, shaped and finished, use a card scraper to remove the paper from the dial area.

The Door: Hang & Fit

The door's position is slightly back from the front edge of the clock, so it's not possible to install butt hinges as you would normally. The leaf mortise on the case side has to be ramped and the barrel of the hinge is on or at the surface.

Establish the mortise locations according to the plan. Mark both the front edge and rear edge of the door. It's from the front edge of the door that you'll ramp the mortise area. The idea is to create a ramp so the hinge leaf is flush to the surface where the outer edge of the leaf meets the case.

To make this ramp, set the inner hinge line with a chisel to a depth equal to the hinge-leaf thickness. At each end of the hinge area, plunge a ⅜" chisel into the waste area while it's set at an approximate

Ramping up a hinge mortise. Installation of the hinges is tricky because the door is slightly recessed into the clock. A ramped mortise allows you to bury the hinge leaf and keep the barrel aligned as needed.

angle that matches the ramp. All that's left is to create the ramp.

Begin with your chisel resting on the outer-most hinge line and slice downward as you move toward the inner layout line. Work slowly until the leaf edge is just flush and the ramp is straight and flat.

Next, install the clock bottom to the hinge side piece. This creates a 90° corner and a place to fit the door. Align the door to the assembled pieces, hold a small gap at the bottom and transfer the hinge location onto the edge of the door.

Because the door thickness matches the length of the hinge leaf, it's possible to cut the recess at a table saw. One method to achieve the necessary depth of cut for the recess is to hold the hinge so the leaves are parallel, measure that thickness, then subtract ¹⁄₁₆" (for a reveal) and set the depth of cut at that figure. I think it's best to install the hinges on the clock body and create a test piece to arrive at the accurate depth of cut.

Once the blade is set for the correct depth of cut, add a tall auxiliary fence to your miter gauge, position

Precise transference. Mark the door-hinge location off the mortises made in the side. Make sure to keep the door aligned as you transfer the layout.

Just like the tenon cuts. Remove the waste from the hinge area on the doors at the table saw. This is the same setup I used to define the tenons for the bottom.

Just like the tenon cuts. Remove the waste from the hinge area on the doors at the table saw. This is the same setup I used to define the tenons for the bottom.

The first of two steps. Form a notch in the supports that will eventually accept the dial back. A number of passes over the saw blade will carve out an area that makes finishing the rabbet a breeze.

the door to cut at the transferred marks and make a pass over the blade with the door clamped to the fence. Cut both ends of the recess on the waste side to define the hinge area; nibble away the balance of the material.

Install the door on the hinges. Add the top to the hinge side/bottom assembly. Mark at the tenon shoulder as well as the baseline of your dovetailed top to establish the exact width of the door. Cutting to that line will make the door fit, but it will be far too tight. Take a look at the reveal at the hinge side and adjust your cut to match.

Finally, turn a door knob from matching hardwood. Form a ⅜" tenon on the end of the knob to fit a ⅜" hole drilled into the door. A small amount of glue secures the knob in place.

Finishing Construction

After you've assembled all the parts of the clock and fit the door to the case, it's time to finalize construction. You have to add supports for the door and dial back, and make then install a backboard.

The two supports pull double duty. First, they act as a stop for the door and second, they hold the plywood dial back. Mill the material for these supports according to the cut sheet. At the table saw, raise the blade height to match the thickness of your plywood dial back. Set the fence to cut at the 7¼" mark. Use

your miter gauge with the auxiliary fence to cut a small notch into each support. Make the first cut with the end of the support tight to the fence, then pull away from the fence making a number of cuts until you've removed about ¾" or more of waste.

Raise the blade to just below its full height. In this position, the cut will be more vertical and the pressure applied from the blade helps hold the stock to the table. Position the fence to rip the area for the dial back, then make the second cut.

The supports are added to the interior of the clock sides, just behind the door. To figure the placement, hold a square to the door and hinge side. Draw a line up both edges of the door. Add a thin bead of glue along the support's length, then attach the support just behind that line with a few small brads.

At this time, if everything is checked and fits, assemble the clock for the last time. Add glue to the dovetails and slip the parts together. I choose not to add glue around the tenons so as not to have any glue squeeze-out to clean up. Besides, the front edge of the tenons gets pegged through the face edge of the sides, which can also be completed as you assemble the clock. And don't forget to cut and fit the plywood dial back. It attaches to the supports with four small screws.

The back on my clock speaks volumes of the builder. Ordinarily, this back would be a piece that's ¼" in

The second of two steps. The support rabbets are finished when you rip the material up to and including the notch. A small amount of waste needs to be cleared prior to the addition of the dial back.

supplies

Woodcraft
woodcraft.com or 800-225-1153

Standard quartz movement
#3723X, $13.99
(includes 4802X hands)

Rare earth magnet
#150950 , $6.49

Rockler
rockler.com or 800-279-4441

Narrow cabinet hinge
#32908, $12.99

Clock Parts
clockparts.com or 888-827-2387

Clock dial; call for pricing

Prices correct at time of publication.

thickness. But because I usually build pieces from the 18th and early 19th centuries, I found myself making this piece as I would a drawer bottom in Queen Anne furniture. If you choose to copy my project, mill the back to size and thickness and set up at the table saw to complete the piece.

Set the fence (with a height extension added) spaced ³⁄₁₆" from the blade, just as a tooth passes below the table's surface. Raise the blade so you can just slide the panel between the blade and the fence. Use a push stick to make the cuts, as shown on the next page. The first cut is at the end grain, while the other two cuts are along the long-grain edges. This results in a near-perfect fit of a backboard into a ¼" groove.

If you choose to make the piece traditionally, mill the back to size and thickness the part to just slip into the groove.

Finish-sand the entire project to #120-grit. There's no need sand go any further unless you plan to use a different finishing method.

The door is held in a closed position with a pair of rare-earth magnets, one in the door and one in a support. After the finish is complete, drill a hole in the support that's sized to accept your magnet. Cut off a small brad, then install the brad into the center of the hole. Close the door onto the brad a few times to mark the location for the second magnet. Install the magnets with a drop or two of thick cyanoacrylate glue and make sure to keep the polarity of the magnets in the correct orientation.

I turned to our resident Arts & Crafts expert, Senior Editor Robert W. Lang, for his help on the finish. He suggested this piece is the perfect size to fume, as was done on period pieces. Fuming involves exposing the wood to ammonia fumes which react with the tannins in the wood to darken its color.

The end result sits proudly on my mantel. I'll bet your results will be equally as impressive.

nine

Voysey Mantel Clock

by ROBERT W. LANG

Charles Francis Annesley Voysey (1857-1941) was one of the eminent architects and designers of the British Arts & Crafts movement of the late 19th and early 20th centuries. Voysey designed complete environments, including textile and wallpaper patterns. His work influenced American designers such as Harvey Ellis, who is also known for the use of architectural details in furniture designs.

The original drawings for this clock are dated 1895, and examples exist in various materials. The best-known of these clocks features a painted bucolic landscape, and a gilded dome and spire. There are also examples in wood, including ebony with ivory inlay and dark oak. There is even a version from 1903 made from aluminum.

For my version, I decided to use contrasting woods, with exotic materials for the inlay. The four legs, dome and spire are tiger maple and the panels and foot mouldings are ebonized walnut. The dots and ring on the face are mother-of-pearl, and the horizontal stripes on the legs are ebony.

Despite the sophisticated appearance of the clock, the case is simple construction: panels fit in stopped grooves in the legs. Where things get tricky is under the top, where the moulding steps in and out around the perimeter. The challenge is one of scale, and finding ways to make the process as simple as possible.

Thin Panels, Tapered Legs

I worked to the original 1895 drawing, and resawed the panels from 4/4 stock. I first made the panels ¹⁄₁₆" thicker than finished size and let them sit for a few days. I piled some scrap lumber on top to help keep them flat, then milled the front, back and sides to ¼" thick and the top to ⁷⁄₃₂" thick. I made the back panel ¼" wider than the finished size to allow for two rips for the back door.

While the panels acclimated, I went to work on the legs, feet and moulding. The legs were milled to 1¼" square, and after deciding which piece of wood looked best in which position, I marked the tops with a cabinetmaker's triangle.

The sequence of tasks on the way from rough blank to finished leg isn't critical. I milled the grooves and cut the stub tenons on the bottoms before cutting the tapers on the outside faces. That – along with the cabinetmaker's triangle – made it easy for me to keep the parts properly oriented.

I set up a ¼" straight bit in the router table, then set the fence and stop-block to make the ¼"-deep grooves

Right-side up. Making the grooves first makes it difficult to mix up the inside and outside of the legs.

Keep it simple. This jig takes only a few minutes to assemble, and provides a safe method to taper the legs at the table saw.

that are ⁹⁄₁₆" from the inside faces and stop 13⁵⁄₁₆" down from the top. That setting works for only one groove on the four legs, so I reset the fence to make the second set of grooves.

With a ⅜"-wide dado stack in the table saw, I set a stop on the miter gauge to make the tenons. After cutting the tenons, I used a simple table saw jig to taper the legs to 1" square at the top, then planed away the saw marks. To complete the legs, use a chisel to square off the ends of the grooves.

Mouldings in Miniature

There are two mouldings used in this piece: a simple ¼"-radius cove on the feet and a more complex profile used as a cornice under the top. Both of these are rather

First on edge. The first cut of the cornice moulding is made with the wood on edge.

Second on face. The final cut leaves the narrow edge at a uniform thickness.

Smooth sailing. A handplane quickly removes the machine marks from the columns and it leaves a flat, smooth surface.

Two easier than four. Each half of a foot is put together, then two pairs are assembled to fit the tenons on the ends of the legs.

small, so I carefully ripped the rough material then brought the pieces to finished size with the planer. I made plenty of blanks about 24" long.

When thin mouldings are mentioned, someone will offer the advice to run the profile on wide pieces then rip the parts to their finished size. Sometimes this makes sense, but with this project it made more sense to me to be careful with the router table setup rather than stop after every pass to move to the table saw and jointer.

That gave me more control over the final size, and took far less time. The key to milling small parts is to use a setup that holds the parts in position as they are cut and keeps fingers out of harm's way.

The foot moulding is made with one pass and a ¼"-radius cove bit, but the ogee moulding requires two setups with different cutters. The ogee is flattened out, so there isn't a standard cutter available that matches the profile. The first cut is made with the moulding on edge, using a portion of a vertical raised-panel bit (Lee Valley #16J63.54). For the second cut, the material is laid flat to pass below a rounded-end grooving bit with a ⅛" radius (Lee Valley #16J42.01).

Make the Cut

There are lots of mitered corners in this project. See "Small Miter Setup" (below) for the two fixtures that I used. I began with the feet, and placed a leg tenon-side up in my vise for reference. I cut one piece of the moulding and when I was satisfied with the length, I made a pencil mark on the base of the miter block and proceeded to cut all 16 pieces of the foot moulding.

After cutting a few pieces, I glued them together in pairs, rubbed the joints and set the pairs aside to dry. With eight pairs completed, I checked the fit of two pairs against the tenon. To adjust the fit, I used my shooting board or, to remove just a tiny bit, rubbed both ends at once against sandpaper glued to scrap plywood. When I was happy with the fit, I glued each foot together. If the assembled foot mortise is a little small, the tenon or the inside of the assembled foot can be filed down.

A Little Off the Top

The top has indented notches, 3" in from each outside corner. It's a nice touch, but the detail that looks simple from above gets complicated down below. There really isn't a way to avoid running the cornice moulding as

One of the challenges of this project is making small miters accurately and efficiently. I made a small miter block to speed the process. Using a table saw or powered miter saw with pieces this small would be insane, but I did use a powered saw to cut a piece of scrap at 45°.

After gluing the three pieces of the miter block together, I clamped the 45° piece to the back fence of the fixture and used it to position my backsaw to make kerfs in the fence to guide the saw through the rest of the project.

I also built a small shooting board to use with my block plane. One piece of plywood serves as a base, and the smaller rectangular piece raises the work into the plane iron. The two narrow fences are aligned

Simple solution. This shop-made miter cutting block (raised to a comfortable height) makes quick work of cutting the numerous miters for this project.

Shoot to fit. This fixture holds the workpiece at the correct angle and guides the block plane to perfect the ends of the mitered pieces.

at 45° to the front edge and are held in place with glue and brads.

Shooting removes a very thin slice from the end of the workpiece. With a sharp plane iron and a bit of wax on the shooting board's base,

it doesn't take long to get a feel for how to hold the wood against the plane and how to adjust the cuts for a good fit.

separate pieces that are mitered at the corners. I used a method that makes it relatively simple, albeit tedious.

The completed top is $5/16$" thick, but Voysey's drawings don't detail how the top attaches to the case, or where the moulding ends and the top begins. It makes sense to run the legs and panels past the bottom edge of the moulding to allow them to cover the transition, yet reduce the thickness of the top.

The top is only $3/32$" thick at the edge – too thin to be practical for the entire part. I realized that a wide rabbet around the perimeter of a thicker top would provide an edge to butt the moulding to as I fit and assembled.

I cut a piece of $1/2$" plywood 2" smaller than the top, and cut a $3/16$"-deep notch 1" in from each corner. Then I cut a second plywood rectangle $3/8$" smaller than the first and attached it to the first piece, aligned with the ends of the $3/16$" notches. I ran a router with a flush-trim bit between the notches to make a pattern the shape of the top, but offset in 1".

I planed the top to $7/32$" thick and cut it to size, then cut a $3/16$"-deep notch 3" in from each outside corner, and made a straight rip from notch to notch at the band saw. Using double-sided tape, I attached the pattern to the bottom of the top then headed to the router table. I installed a straight bit with a bearing above the cutter and set the height to leave $3/32$" at the edge of the top.

It took several passes to cut the rabbet because the bit diameter is smaller than the width of the rabbet. I made the first pass as a climb-cut to create a nice edge without tear-out, bracing the piece against the router table fence to keep it under control. The last pass was with the bearing against the template.

Multitude of Miters

With the top bottom-side up near my miter block, I began to fit the moulding to the inner notches. The rabbet made it easy to set one end against the inside corner so I could mark the other. With the four inside pieces cut, it was time to deal with the small return pieces.

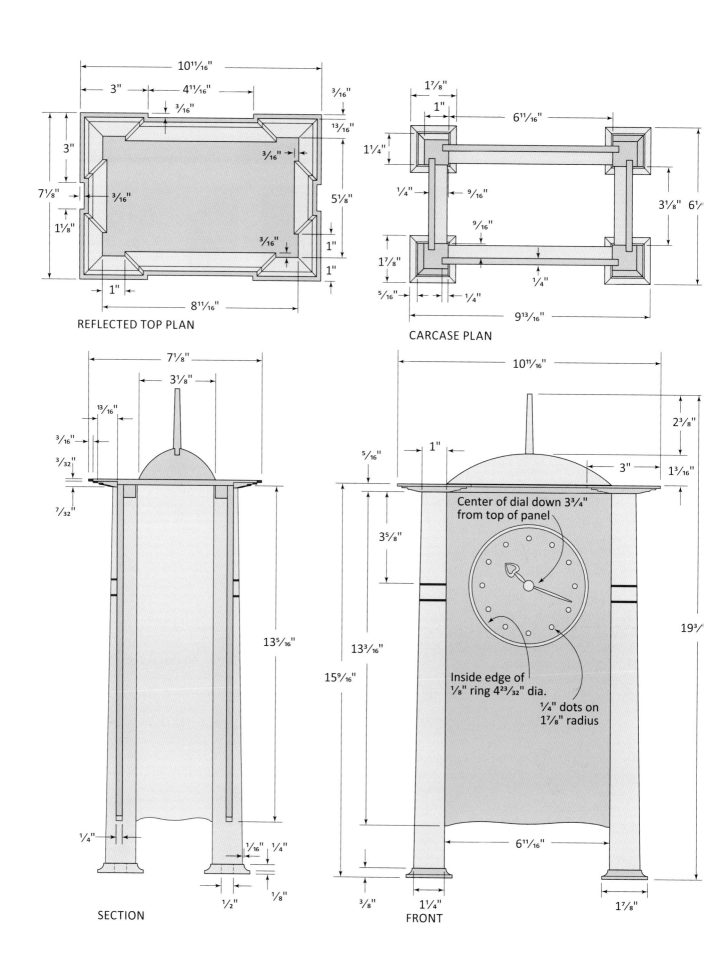

REFLECTED TOP PLAN

CARCASE PLAN

SECTION

FRONT

Center of dial down 3³⁄₄"
from top of panel

Inside edge of
¹⁄₈" ring 4²³⁄₃₂" dia.

¹⁄₄" dots on
1⁷⁄₈" radius

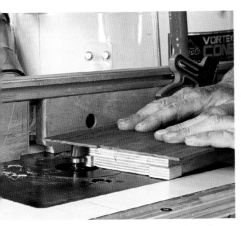

Follow me. The pattern is made to the exact size of the perimeter rabbet. The bearing on the bit follows the pattern to make the cut.

Start inside. The rabbet provides exact locations for the cornice moulding. The first piece fits within the notch.

Slight return. The outside corners are used to mark the length of the moulding returns after the first miter is fit.

I shot one end of each return piece, cut it to rough length and glued it to a long piece; by the time the last piece was cut and glued, the first was dry. I then used the shooting board and block plane to trim to my pencil marks.

For each outside corner, I cut and assembled two pieces. The final assembly of the top's moulding was made easier by dealing with eight sub-assemblies instead of 20 individual pieces.

For Appearance's Sake

The inlays on the face are mother-of-pearl, available pre-cut from online suppliers to luthiers. The 1/8"-wide ring is made for the sound hole of a guitar, and the 1/4"-diameter dots are fingerboard markers. The location of the inlays is based on the clock face.

The inner diameter of the ring is 120mm, or slightly more than 4²³⁄₃₂". I made a disc from 1/2" plywood, 1/2" smaller than that size, and attached it to the front panel with double-sided tape and a screw through the center and into my bench. With a 1/8"-diameter straight bit in a small plunge router with a 5/8"-diameter guide collar, I routed the recess for the ring.

The dots are laid out on a 3¾"-diameter circle. I drew vertical and horizontal centerlines, then drew the circle with my compass. That radius equals one-

Voysey Mantel Clock

NO.	ITEM	DIMENSIONS (INCHES)			MATERIAL
		T	W	L	
4	Legs	1¼	1¼	15¼	Tiger maple
1	Front panel	¼	7³⁄₁₆	13⁵⁄₁₆	Ebonized walnut
2	Side panels	¼	3⅝	13⁵⁄₁₆	Ebonized walnut
1	Back panel	¼	7⁷⁄₁₆*	13⁹⁄₁₆	Ebonized walnut
1	Foot moulding	⅜	⁹⁄₁₆	48	Ebonized walnut
1	Top panel	⁷⁄₃₂	7⅛	10¹¹⁄₁₆	Ebonized walnut
1	Top moulding	⁷⁄₃₂	¹³⁄₁₆	72	Ebonized walnut
1	Dome	1³⁄₁₆	3⅛	6¹¹⁄₁₆	Tiger maple**
1	Spire	⁵⁄₁₆	⁵⁄₁₆	2⅝	Tiger maple†
16	Column inlays	⅛	⅜	1⁹⁄₁₆	Ebony
1	Hour hand	¹⁄₁₆	⁹⁄₁₆	1⁹⁄₁₆	Tiger maple**
1	Minute hand	¹⁄₁₆	⁹⁄₁₆	2¼	Tiger maple**

*Larger than front panel to allow back door cutout; **Cut to pattern; †Tenon one end (¼" long)

Handle it. The smallest pieces are glued to longer ones to make it possible to hold them for trimming the ends to the exact length.

Happy ending. The outer corners are the last to be fit (and are the easiest to adjust) to complete the cornice moulding.

Take a turn. A plywood circle is used as a template for the router guide collar to follow when making the groove for the inlaid ring.

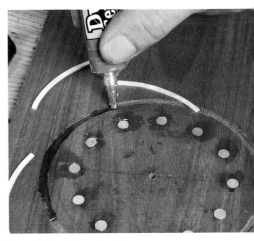

Drop in. The inlay materials were purchased as pre-cut parts from a luthier's supply store. These parts could also be fabricated from wood or other materials.

supplies

Klockit
klockit.com or 800-556-2548

Q-80 quartz clock movement
#10082, $6.99

Flat hand
#66943, $.79

Sweep second hand
#68047, $.79

Duke Luthier
dukeluthier.com

120mm guitar rosette
#MOP 3mm rosette, $9.95

Stewart-MacDonald
stewmac.com or 800-848-2273

¼" Pearl dots (12)
#0011, $.67 each

Lee Valley
leevalley.com or 800-871-8158

20mm x 13mm hinges (1 pair)
#00D30.04, $1.40

Prices correct at time of publication.

sixth of the circumference so I stepped off the location of half the dots from the intersection of the vertical centerline and the circle, and the other half from the horizontal centerline.

The shallow holes for the pre-cut dots are made with a Forstner bit at the drill press. I aimed to set the mother-of-pearl slightly below the surface of the wood. That is ideal, but it's not critical because the inlay can be sanded with common woodworking abrasives. Duco cement holds the inlays in place.

Around the Back
A small door on the back panel on the original accesses the clockworks; a small knob and wooden keeper hold it shut. I marked the location of the door, drew reference marks across the panel then made two rip cuts at the table saw to create the stiles. That was followed by two crosscuts to form the rails.

I installed the hinges on the door and the right-hand stile before gluing the panel back together. The hinges are tiny, so I made the gains for them by slicing the ends with a knife and "routing" the depth with my marking gauge.

At this point I made a test assembly, fitting each panel between two legs and testing the fit on the inside of the top panel. I made a couple of adjustments as needed by planing the edges of the panels or scraping away the back of the moulding. When each panel fit individually, I assembled all four with the legs and made sure everything fit neatly within the moulding.

Four ½"-square cleats were cut from scrap to fit in between the legs; I simply glued them to the top,

One at a time. Each panel is fit to the top before attempting to fit the entire carcase. That makes it easy to find the troublemakers.

Perfect match. The back door is cut with four straight cuts from a single panel; the hinges are installed before reassembly.

taking care not to get any glue on the panels. I then took the case apart to make the dome and spire, and to inlay the horizontal bands on the legs.

The slots for the dark bands are made at the table saw. I raised the blade to match the distance from the outer edge of the groove to the face of the leg at the top band and made a cut across each of the tapered faces. The slot for the lower band needs to be slightly deeper, so I used the edge of a file to adjust the slot. The goal is to leave the bands barely proud of the show surface and trim them flush later.

These inlays are genuine ebony, as opposed to the ebonized walnut for the panels and moulding. The ebonizing solution reacts with the maple, so these inlays can't be stained after they are in place. I milled some ebony to match the width of the slots, and ripped them slightly wider than necessary. I mitered the outer corners and glued them in place, then trimmed them flush with my block plane after the glue was dry.

Hold on there. Square cleats glued to the bottom of the top capture the panels. Final assembly comes after the panels are ebonized and the columns are oiled.

A Dome of Your Own

After printing a full-size drawing of the front and side arcs for the dome, I used spray adhesive to attach the paper to the dome blank. There is a small flat square at the top of the dome to mate with the bottom of the spire. I cut a 3/16"-square mortise with a drill bit and a square punch, about 1/4" deep.

Because the curves go entirely to the bottom edge of the dome, I temporarily attached a 1½"-square block to the blank with double-sided tape. I made the vertical cut first, then used blue painter's tape to put the scraps back on the blank. Then I made the cuts in the other

One, two, three. Rasps remove the band saw marks, refine the shape and smooth the surface of the dome.

Nothing yet. The ebonizing solution won't change the color immediately. The chemical reaction between the rusty vinegar and the tannic acid in the wood takes a few minutes.

Inlay-safe. The solution has no effect on the mother-of-pearl inlay. Residue from coloring is removed with a non-woven abrasive pad, then the panel is ready for assembly.

direction. The bulk of the saw marks were removed with rasps before finish-sanding the dome.

The spire starts as a ⁵⁄₁₆"-square piece, and I used the full-size drawing to lay out the tapers and the teeny tenon. The shoulders of the tenon were cut with a backsaw, then I used a chisel to pare down the cheeks. The taper was made with a block plane.

Time on my Hands

The inexpensive quartz movement mounts to the clock at the center of the face. These movements are nice, but the metal hands that come with them are not – so I decided to make ¹⁄₁₆"-thick wood hands, and attach those to the standard-issue metal ones. Using the metal hands as a backing allowed me to easily mount the wooden ones.

My first attempt at cutting hands with the scrollsaw failed; the wood split at the heart-shaped cutout of the hour hand. I tried again, this time using three thicknesses glued in a stack with contact cement. This survived the session at the scrollsaw, and after shaping the hands with a file, I separated the strips by pouring a little lacquer thinner on the edge of the stack.

After trimming the metal hands to size and roughing the surface with sandpaper, I epoxied the metal hands to the back of the wood ones, let the epoxy cure, then pared the circular end of the minute hand with a chisel to provide room for the nut to thread securely.

Color with Chemistry

Good old American walnut can be colored to a dramatic black with a home-brew solution. I put a pint of vinegar in a plastic cup, tossed in a ripped-up pad of steel wool and let that soak for a few days. (Gas forms as the acid in the vinegar works on the metal, so leave the container open; if you cap it, it can explode.) The liquid remains clear, but the metal starts to dissolve and scum forms on the surface. Before using the solution, strain it through a coffee filter into another container.

When you brush the liquid on the walnut, nothing happens at first. A chemical reaction between the tannins in the wood and the solution changes the color, and that takes a few minutes.

When the wood dries out, there may be some residue on the surface. The rusty vinegar doesn't react with the mother-of-pearl, so I only needed to wipe off the sludge after coloring. I buffed the surfaces of the panels with a nylon abrasive pad to remove the residue and to smooth the surfaces.

The walnut may look more blue than black, but the application of clear shellac (or other clear finish) delivers a nice dark color. The figured maple on the legs is accented with a coat of clear Danish oil applied before final assembly.

My last step before putting the clock together permanently was to locate and drill two holes through the underside of the top and into the dome.

Together at Last

With the top upside down on the bench, I ran a bead of liquid hide glue down each groove, then put the panels in the grooves. I then ran a bead of glue in the corner where the cleats meet the top and set the assembled legs and panels in place.

After making sure that everything was in the right position and after gluing the spire into the dome, I left the parts to dry overnight. The following day, I flipped the assembly over and permanently attached the dome by reaching in through the back door to drive the two screws.

The assembled clock was sprayed with four coats of clear shellac (on a small project such as this, you can use the stuff in the spray cans). After allowing the shellac to dry completely, I sanded the surface with #320-grit sandpaper, followed by an abrasive pad. A coat of satin lacquer, also from a spray can, completed the finish.

ten

Tusk-Tenon Bookrack

by ROBERT W. LANG

This small bookrack can be made entirely by using hand tools, or entirely by using machines – I used both.

The key elements in this project are the through tenons that connect the shelf to the ends. I based the design on an early 20th century example from the Roycroft community. It's an ideal way to learn this method of joinery – it only takes a few board feet of material and each step is an opportunity to improve your skills.

A project like this is enjoyable if the parts go together with a minimum amount of fuss. That means that the mortises and tenons need to be in the right places, and at the right sizes.

I used a pair of templates and a router with a flush-trimming bit to locate and size the joints. This way, the work of getting things to fit has to be done only once, when making the templates. Work on the real parts goes quickly and if I want to make this piece again, or make a batch of them, I'm well on my way before I even begin building.

The patterns are made from ½" Baltic birch plywood. MDF would also work, but the plywood's edges hold up better over time. You can enlarge the drawing on page 70 or you can download a full-size version on our web site popularwoodworking.com/aug07 and print it yourself. Before cutting the outer shape, lay out and make the mortises.

There are many possible ways to make the mortises. I used a ⅝"-diameter straight bit in a plunge router, guided by the router's fence. With the pattern blank firmly clamped to my bench I plunged the router within my layout lines to make the cut.

Make the Templates

The advantage of the router is that it removes a lot of material quickly, making smooth mortises with parallel sides. The disadvantage is that it can't make a mortise with square ends. But two hand tools – the chisel and the rasp – solve this problem quickly. First on the template and then on the real parts.

Because I had to square the rounded ends of the mortise slots by hand, I didn't bother setting any stops for the ends of the mortises. I did it by eye, starting and stopping about ¹⁄₁₆" inside the lines.

After chopping away most of the waste in the corners with the chisel, finish the mortises with a rasp. With those done, cut the outer shape of the pattern with the band saw or jigsaw, and smooth the perimeter

Form and function. The first template generates the shape of the ends and the through mortises. The oak blank below it is cut ¹⁄₁₆" oversize, and the holes minimize the work for the router bit.

Guided by the kerf. One precise cut establishes the size of the tenon. This L-shaped jig attached to the miter gauge is simple and safe.

Nothing to chance. The saw kerf in the horizontal part of the jig shows exactly where the blade will cut. With the layout line at the kerf line, clamp the piece to the jig.

Built-in guidance system. The flat area of the routed mortise acts as a guide for the back of the chisel. Rest the back against the cut and swing the edge of the chisel down to the corner (left). This shallow line will guide the tool in the next step of making the cut. With the edge of the chisel in the line, push straight down. Clean up both end-grain surfaces of the mortise and then finish the cut on the ends. The long-grain cuts tend to split, so shave off a little at a time (right). A few strokes with a rasp will finish the mortises.

Get this right and success will follow. Take time to fit the tenons in the shelf template to the mortises in the end pattern. When the parts are routed to the templates, the joints will work.

with the rasp before adding the stops. A dab of glue and a couple 23-gauge pins hold the stops in place.

The shelf template is made from the template for the ends. Line up one edge of the shelf pattern blank to the end of one of the mortises in the other template and transfer mortise locations. The ⅜" offset in the shelf pattern allows space for the edge that will be added to the back of the shelf after the bookrack is assembled.

Make the cuts that define the edges of the tenons on the table saw. To do this, screw a couple pieces of scrap together in an "L" shape and attach that to the miter gauge of the table saw. This provides a reference for where the blade will be during the cut.

Clamp the shelf pattern to the miter gauge attachment to hold it in position and to keep your hands a safe distance from the blade during the cut.

To remove the waste between the tenons, make a rough cut on the waste side of the layout lines at the band saw then clamp a straight piece of plywood directly on the line. Then, with a flush-cutting bit in a router, trim the pattern back to the line and clean up the corners with a chisel. The goal at this point is to get the tenons on the shelf pattern to fit in width in the mortises of the end pattern, as seen above.

When pattern-trimming mortises in solid wood parts like this, I always use the smallest diameter router bit available. This minimizes the curved waste left in the inside corners. I use the patterns to trace the shapes on the wood. I keep close to, but just outside the lines to reduce the material the router will remove. Then I cut all the parts to rough sizes.

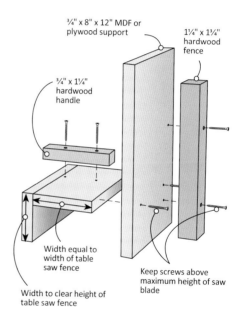

¾" x 8" x 12" MDF or plywood support

¾" x 1¼" hardwood handle

1¼" x 1¾" hardwood fence

Width equal to width of table saw fence

Keep screws above maximum height of saw blade

Width to clear height of table saw fence

A simple tenoning jig. A tenoning jig such as this one can help you cut the shoulders on your through tenons. Add a clamp above the highest position of the saw blade as shown below, and screw it in place. Adjust the arm on the clamp to firmly hold the material.

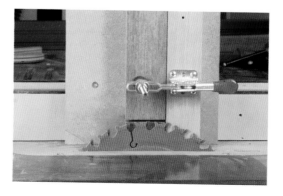

Good Reason to Go Backward

Hogging off a lot of solid wood is an invitation to chipping or tearing out the solid wood, particularly on the curves. Clamp the patterns and the parts securely to your bench and make the first pass moving the router counterclockwise around the outside of the pattern. Climb cutting in this way helps to reduce chipping and tear-out. Drill two holes at the mortise locations to allow the bearing on the bit to reach the pattern below.

After routing the mortises, the corners have to be squared. I use a chisel and put the back against the end-grain edge of the straight part of the mortise. Holding the chisel flush, swing the corner down to establish a straight line.

Turn the chisel 90° to set the perpendicular line at the end of the mortise. Then, go back to the end-grain side and force the chisel down as far as possible, cutting across the grain. After cutting the two opposite end-grain faces, make paring cuts with the grain.

The tenons will fit in the width of the mortise – or at least be very close – from the template. To get them to fit in thickness, and to establish a shoulder on the inside of the joint, trim half the difference in thickness off each cheek of the tenon, using a tenoning jig.

Before fitting the tenons, chamfer the ends. This makes starting the tenons in the mortises easier, and it prevents the tenon from doing any damage on the way out of the other side of the mortise. Start the ends in the mortises and push down. If they stop, look to see which face of the tenon should be trimmed.

Tight But Not Too Tight

Aim for a snug fit. It's right when you can force the first part of the tenon into the mortise by hand, and are able to lift both pieces without the joint coming apart. Take a few licks with a card scraper or rasp to remove the saw and router marks from the tenon.

Insurance before fitting. Chamfering the ends of the through tenons before fitting them makes them easier to start in the mortises and prevents damage on the way out of the other side.

Cutting the shoulders. Use a tenoning jig such as the one shown on page 67 to make the shoulder cuts on the through tenons. The clamp on the far end holds the workpiece to the jig.

This loosens the joint just enough to get it almost all the way home with hand pressure. A few taps with a dead-blow mallet seats the shoulder of the joint. Mark a pencil line where the cheek of the tenon meets the face of the end piece. After all the work of putting the joint together, it's time to take it apart again to make the small mortises for the tusks.

The tusks pull the tenon into the mortise by bearing on the face of the mortised end. Locating the back of the mortise just behind the face ensures this. After offsetting the pencil line on the tenon 1/16" back, mark out a square, centered mortise and cut it with one stroke of a 1/2" chisel on the hollow-chisel mortiser. A block of scrap under the tenon holds it above the machine's table and prevents the back side from tearing out as the chisel exits. This mortise could, of course, be made by drilling a 3/8" or 7/16" hole and squaring the corners with a chisel if a mortising machine isn't available.

Taking Aim on the Angle

The outer edge of the mortise is sloped about 1/16" in the thickness of the tenon to match the angle on the tusks. This wedging action locks the joint together and if the tusks loosens from wood shrinkage, gravity or a tap on top will tighten the joint.

Holding the back of the chisel against the long-grain sides of the small mortise, swing the edge of the chisel down to nick the corners at the layout line.

Testing the fit. Fine adjustments of the saw's fence allow a good fit. The tenon can be pushed in with hand pressure, and the mortised end can be lifted without falling.

Then, place the edge of the chisel on the line and push straight down. Don't push hard – just enough to make an incision along the pencil line. The edge of the chisel will fit in this slit; tilt the handle of the chisel toward you. Looking down the handle, aim for the edge at the bottom of the mortise. With the chisel in position, a few taps with a mallet make the slanted cut on the inside of the mortise.

To make the tusks, mill some scrap slightly thicker than the ½" mortise and about ⅞" wide. Make lengths

Eyeing the angle. Set the chisel on the line and lean the chisel back until the edge is in line with the bottom of the mortise. Strike the chisel with a mallet to complete the cut.

Just a bit behind. The back edge of the second through mortise is back from the face of the end $\frac{1}{16}$". The tusk will then be able to pull the joint tight.

that are roughly two tusks long plus 1", and plane the tusks until they fit the mortise in width. Lay out two tusks, cut them to shape on the band saw then drive one end into the mortise.

The excess length on the tusks gives some room to fiddle with the fit of the angled tusks in the slanted mortise. A rasp followed by a card scraper removes the band-saw marks on the tusks. When the fit is good, mark the bottom of the tusks ¼" up from the bottom of the end and ¾" above the top cheek of the tenon.

Then mark the final outline of the tusks, trim them with the band saw and finish shaping with a rasp. When all four tusks fit, take the entire piece apart one last time to scrape and sand the surfaces. Sand the wide surfaces and exposed edges, but stay away from the through tenons and parts of the tusks that fit in the small mortises.

To Glue or Not to Glue

The original version of the bookrack was shipped in a flat carton, and assembled by the purchaser. Glue is an option, but not a necessity, to hold the tusk joints together. The joints are surprisingly strong on their own.

After final assembly, the exposed parts of the tenons and tusks are scraped and sanded. While quartersawn white oak is tough to cut, it is easy to sand. I generally go over the entire piece with a card scraper and only sand with #150 or #180-grit sandpaper.

The back edge of the shelf is the last piece attached. After cutting it to size and sanding it, run a bead of glue along the edge of the shelf, and hold the edge to the shelf with a few clamps, then let the glue dry overnight.

I usually put a darker finish on pieces like this, but every now and then I like to see a piece without any added color. On this shelf, I used two coats of amber shellac. After letting the shellac dry thoroughly, scuff it with a Scotch-Brite pad and apply a coat of paste wax.

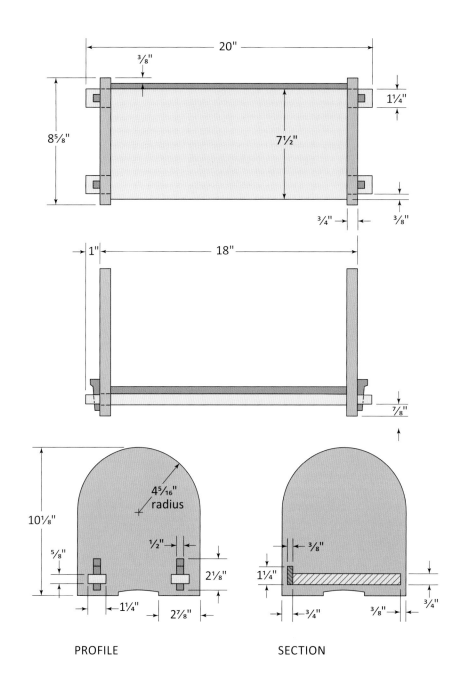

PROFILE

SECTION

Tusk-Tenon Bookrack

NO.	ITEM	DIMENSIONS (INCHES)			MATERIAL	COMMENTS
		T	W	L		
2	Ends	³/₄	8⁵/₈	10¹/₈	QSWO*	Cut big, rout to size
1	Shelf	³/₄	7¹/₂	20	QSWO*	
4	Keys	¹/₂	⁷/₈	2¹/₈	QSWO*	Cut from longer piece
1	Shelf edge	³/₈	1¹/₄	16¹/₂	QSWO*	

*Quartersawn white oak

Shelving & Storage

eleven

Traditional
Hanging Shelves

by TROY SEXTON

These shelves are quite popular with my two best customers: my wife and my daughter. We have them hanging in several rooms of our farmhouse where they hold plates and knickknacks.

Not surprisingly, these shelves are also popular with my paying customers. While many of them may dream of buying a custom corner cupboard, sometimes what they can best afford are the hanging shelves. So these small projects make everyone happy.

For the home woodworker, these shelves are a home run. These two traditional designs look great in most homes, and the woodworking part is so simple that almost anyone should be able to build these in a weekend.

Patterns & Dados

Both of these shelves are built using the same techniques and joints. The only significant difference is that the Shaker-style unit has three shelves and the 18th century "Whale Tail" project has four shelves and a more ornate profile that looks vaguely like a whale's tail. To me, it looks more like a goose.

Begin your project by selecting your lumber and planing it down to ½" thick. Using the supplied patterns and the construction drawings, draw the profile on your side pieces and mark where the dados should go.

Now set up your dado stack in your table saw so it makes a ½"-wide cut that's ³⁄₁₆" deep. As you can see in the photo, I made this cut using only the fence. I feel very comfortable with this cut; but if you're not, I recommend you use your miter gauge and a stop block attached to your fence to guide the work instead.

Cut the dados and then head for the band saw.

Cutting the Details

I use a band saw to shape the sides. Begin by making several "relief" cuts along the profile of your side. These allow you to remove the waste in chunks so your blade and workpiece are easier to maneuver through the cut.

Once you've completed both sides, sand the edges using a drum sander that's chucked into your drill press. I recommend you tape the two sides together using double-sided tape and sand them simultaneously. It's faster and the sides end up identical.

Once that's complete, fit the shelves and sides together for a dry fit. Notice anything? The square edges of the shelves don't match the sides exactly.

Mark the shape of the sides onto the end of the shelves. Now, using a jointer with the fence beveled (or

Cut the dados in the sides using a dado stack in your table saw. If you're a beginning woodworker, I recommend you perform this operation with a miter gauge to guide the work instead of the fence. I've made a lot of these shelves and am quite comfortable with this method.

Relief cut

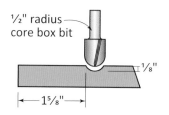

½" radius
core box bit

⅛"

1⅝"

PLATE RAIL GROOVE DETAIL

a handplane), shape the front edge to match the side. You just want to get in the ballpark; sanding can take care of the rest of the contouring job.

Now cut the plate rail groove in the shelves. I used a router bit with a core box profile and a router table. The plate rail is ⅛" deep and 1⅝" in from the back edge.

Before you assemble the unit, finish sand all the surfaces except the outside of the sides. Begin with #100-grit sandpaper and work your way up to #120, #150 and finish with #180.

Assembly & Finishing

Put a small bead of glue in each dado and put the shelves in place. Clamp the shelves between the sides and check your project to make sure it's square by measuring diagonally from corner to corner. If the measurements are equal, nail the sides to the shelves using a few 18-gauge brads.

If your measurements aren't equal, clamp the project diagonally from one corner to another. Clamp across the two corners that produced the longest measurement. Apply a little pressure to those corners and keep checking your diagonal measurements. When they are equal, nail the project together.

After an hour, take the project out of the clamps and sand the outside of the side pieces and putty your nail holes. Ease all the sharp edges of the project using #120-grit sandpaper. I dyed my project using a water-based aniline dye that I mixed myself from several custom colors. I recommend you use J.E. Moser's Golden Amber Maple dye for a similar effect. It's available from Woodworker's Supply at 800-645-9292 or woodworker.com.

Finally, add a couple coats of your favorite top-coat finish and sand between coats. Hang your shelf using some common picture hooks, available at any home center.

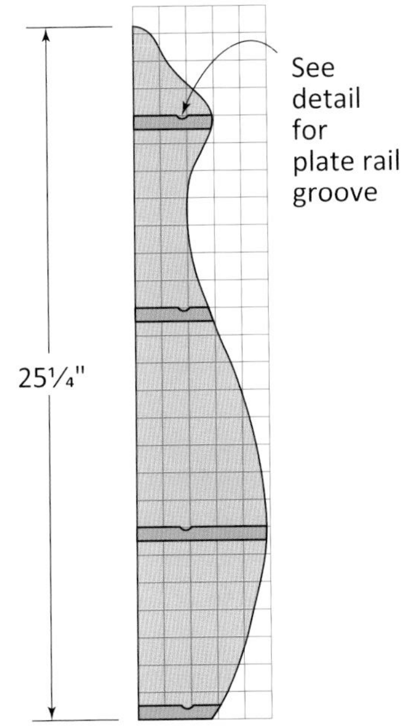

25¼"
See detail for plate rail groove

SECTION
1" GRID

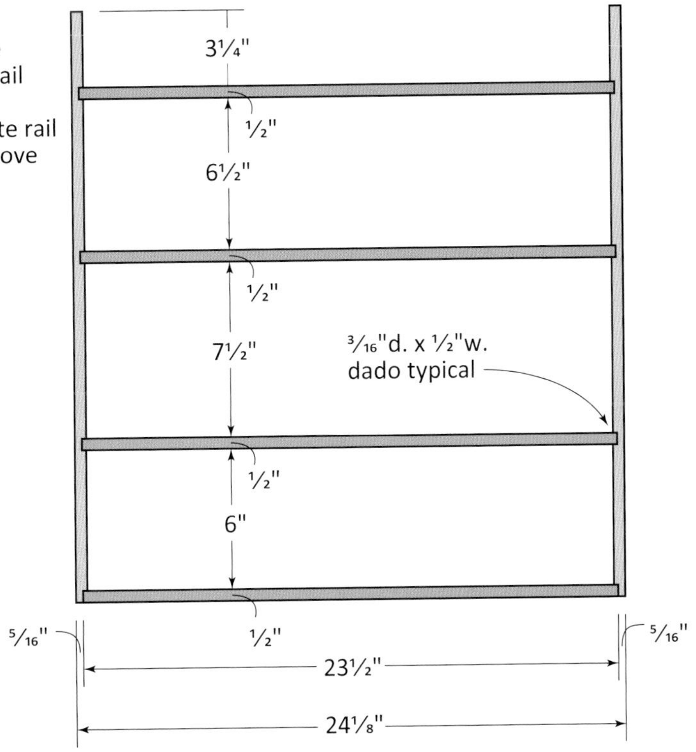

3¼"
½"
6½"
½"
7½"
3/16"d. x ½"w. dado typical
½"
6"
½"
5/16"
5/16"
23½"
24⅛"

ELEVATION

Whale Tail Shelf

NO.	ITEM	DIMENSIONS (INCHES) T	W	L	MATERIAL	COMMENTS
2	Sides	½	4⅞	25¼	Maple	
1	Bottom shelf	½	3⅛	23½	Maple	in 3/16" x ½" dado
1	Middle shelf	½	4⅞	23½	Maple	in 3/16" x ½" dado
1	Middle shelf	½	3	23½	Maple	in 3/16" x ½" dado
1	Top shelf	½	3	23½	Maple	in 3/16" x ½" dado

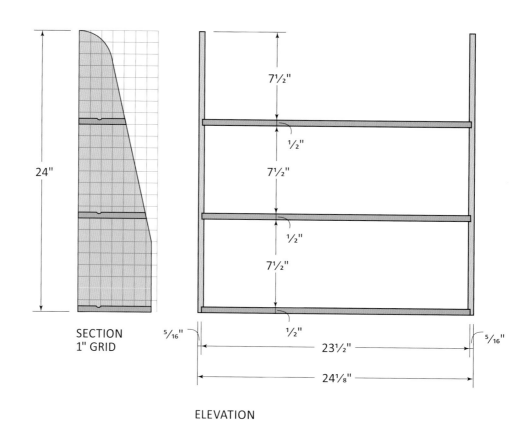

SECTION
1" GRID

ELEVATION

Shaker Hanging Shelf

NO.	ITEM	DIMENSIONS (INCHES)			MATERIAL	COMMENTS
		T	W	L		
2	Sides	½	6½	24	Cherry	
1	Bottom shelf	½	6½	23½	Cherry	in ³⁄₁₆" x ½" dado
1	Middle shelf	½	6	23½	Cherry	in ³⁄₁₆" x ½" dado
1	Top shelf	½	4¼	23½	Cherry	in ³⁄₁₆" x ½" dado

twelve

Bent Lamination Shelves

by ROBERT W. LANG

Most of the time when a piece of wood has a bend or a curve, it means trouble: Your stock is warped or bowed. But sometimes a bent part can add an interesting design element. The curved supports in these shelves transform what might be plain and ordinary into an interesting and contemporary design.

I usually like to keep things simple, which to me means using as few parts as possible. But when it comes to curved parts, such as the supports for these shelves, I form the curves by gluing together several thin strips rather than steam bending one piece of wood. This technique of bent lamination is faster and the results are more predictable than steam bending.

With steam bending, you need a boiler, a steam box and a way to quickly clamp a scalding-hot piece of wood to a form. Then you need to wait several days for the part to dry. With bent lamination you need only a form and a way to clamp the thin strips of wood to it. You don't need to wait an hour or more for the wood to get ready to bend and you don't need to race like a madman to get a hot piece of wood clamped in place. Once the glue is thoroughly dry, the parts are ready to use.

The techniques I used to build these shelves can be employed many different ways. Table aprons and chair backs are common uses for curved parts. Once the shape and size of the curve is determined, you build a form for gluing, and decide what thickness of strips to use to make the curved parts.

Make an Educated Guess

I like to use the thickest strips possible to minimize the number of parts and glue lines. The more strips in the lamination however, the stronger it will be, and the likelihood of the curve springing back away from the form will be minimized.

To get the finished thickness of ¾", I could use four strips ³⁄₁₆" thick, six strips ⅛" thick, eight strips ³⁄₃₂" thick or a dozen pieces ¹⁄₁₆" thick. It all depends on what wood is used and how tight the radius of the curve is.

I make a good guess at a thickness, and resaw a piece of the material to that size. I then bend the piece to roughly the curve I want. If it's difficult to bend, or I hear any popping or cracking noises as I make the bend, I try again with a slightly thinner piece. For this project, which uses ash, I started at ³⁄₁₆" thickness but ultimately decided to use ⅛" for the strips to make the shelf supports.

The next step is to build the form used for bending the curved parts. The shelf supports finish at 2" wide, but the laminations are glued together at 2½". The extra width means I don't have to worry about keeping all of the edges perfectly lined up during gluing. After the glue has dried overnight, I can get a clean edge on the jointer, and achieve the final width by ripping the part on the table saw. One more light cut on the jointer will remove any saw marks. A few quick swipes with a card scraper leave the edges ready for finishing.

To get the 2¼" thickness for the form, I used three layers of ¾"-thick birch plywood cut to the inside radius of the curve, and a fourth piece as a base plate. It doesn't matter what the form is made from; I used material that was left over from another project. I would have used particleboard or medium-density fiberboard (MDF) if I had found a piece of that first.

Instead of making a giant compass, I draw the curve by bending a thin strip of wood across the layout marks. Finish nails hold the shape while I mark the curve with a pencil.

After smoothing the first piece, rough-cut parts are then added to the form. A flush-trimming bit is used in the router to make identical curves for the bending form.

The radius is 56$\frac{11}{16}$", which would require a long trammel to draw and cut the curve. Instead, I simply marked the end points and centerline of the curve, and marked off the 4" rise at the center. I then drove a 4d finish nail at each of these points, and bent a thin strip of wood across them.

It takes three hands to bend and mark the curve. If you don't have someone to help you, drive finishing nails at an angle close to the points used to define the curve. With the midpoint inside the nail, and the ends outside, the thin piece will hold its shape. You can bend the nails to position it exactly where you want it. I cut the curve on the band saw, being careful to saw just outside the pencil line. Then I used #80-grit sandpaper wrapped on a block of wood to get the curved edge smooth.

The First Part is the Pattern

The first layer of the pattern is the only one that requires this much work. The remaining pattern pieces can be marked by tracing the first one. After cutting them slightly oversize, they are attached to the first piece with half-a-dozen #8 x 1¼" screws, and the edges are trimmed with a flush-cutting bit in the router.

After attaching the base plate, the surfaces of the form were given a couple coats of paste wax to keep glue from sticking to them.

Now make the strips for the laminations. They can be ripped on the table saw, but it can be dangerous to work with parts that thin, and nearly half of the material will be lost to the saw kerf. By using the band saw, the operation is much safer and less material is wasted. I cut the strips to ³⁄₁₆" and took them down to the finished thickness of ⅛" by sending them through the thickness planer. I clamped a piece of scrap MDF to the planer bed to carry the thin pieces. Because the ash I used was straight grained, I didn't worry about the edge grain matching, and cut all the strips I needed from 4/4 stock.

In addition to cutting the strips wider than they need to be, I also cut the strips about 6" longer. When you glue six pieces together at a time, they can slide around some, and each layer is slightly shorter than the layer next to it. It's easier to leave them long and trim them when you're done.

Get Ready to Glue

Before attempting a glue-up, I made a dry run to make sure my clamping method would work, and that

Resawing strips on the band saw is safer and less wasteful than using the table saw. I cut them a little thicker than necessary, clean up the saw marks, and bring them to final thickness with the planer.

Thin pieces can be sent through the planer on a sled, a piece of ¾"-thick MDF that extends past the feed rollers and is clamped to the planer bed.

Polyurethane glue can be messy as it cures. I use a thin bead of glue and spread it out with a putty knife to avoid this.

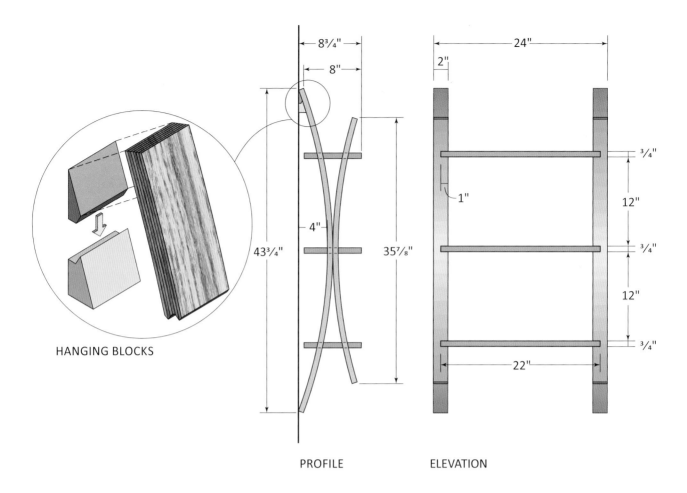

HANGING BLOCKS

PROFILE

ELEVATION

everything I needed was at hand. To form a fair curve, pressure must be evenly applied. This means a lot of clamps placed closely together. During the dry run I determined that 4" or 5" apart was a good spacing.

Typically I use yellow glue for most of my woodworking but bent lamination isn't a standard process. The wood wants to straighten back out, and yellow glue is somewhat flexible after it's dry. A glue that dries more rigidly should be used. Epoxy, plastic resin and reactive polyurethane all dry to a rigid line. I chose to use polyurethane (Gorilla Glue) because it doesn't need to be mixed before using.

I laid the strips out in order, and put a thin bead of glue down the middle of each strip. I then used a putty knife to spread out the bead evenly across each strip. I stacked the strips back up, and placed them in the form. I started clamping in the center, and worked out to the ends, alternating right and left.

Each lamination was left in the clamps for four hours to dry. After removing the bent part from the form, I scraped off the excess glue. After the last part was removed from the form, I waited another 24 hours to be sure that the glue was fully cured before moving on to the next step.

I cleaned up one edge of each curved piece on the jointer. I then carefully ripped each part to $\frac{1}{32}$" over the finished width on the table saw. This can be done safely by keeping the part flat against the table and tight against the fence at the infeed edge of the saw blade. After this cut, I returned to the jointer and removed the saw marks with one pass over the machine's cutterhead.

Form Does Double Duty

To make the ¾"-wide x 1"-deep notches in the supports, I put them back in the gluing jig. I added spacers below them to keep the top of each piece flush with the top of the jig. I added guide strips to the form to guide my router when cutting the notches. To prevent making two lefts and no rights, I didn't trim the ends to their final lengths until all the ¾" notches were cut and the pairs of curves were glued together.

I marked the center 2" of each piece and planed a flat in this area with my block plane. I clamped pairs of curves together, using scraps of wood to keep the notches aligned and in the same plane. After the glue had dried overnight, I marked the ends of the uprights from locations marked on the bending form and trimmed the ends with a handsaw.

Starting at the center and working out to each end, clamps are placed every 4" to 5" around the form.

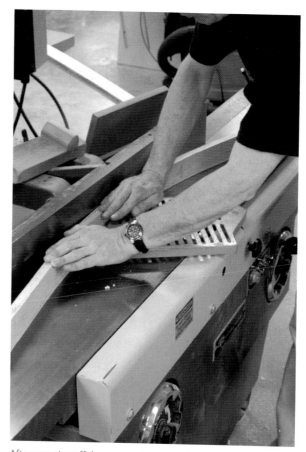

After scraping off the excess glue, one edge is evened up on the jointer. Make sure to keep the curve in contact with the fence on the outfeed side of the cutterhead.

Bent Lamination Shelves

NO.	ITEM	DIMENSIONS (INCHES)			MATERIAL	COMMENTS
		T	W	L		
2	Rear supports	¾	2½*	54*	Ash	From 12 ⅛" pieces
2	Front supports	¾	2½*	54*	Ash	From 12 ⅛" pieces
3	Shelves	¾	8	22	Ash	
4	Hanging blocks	1	1½	1¾	Ash	Cut from larger block

*Sizes reflect overage for trimming

I used my smoothing plane to fine-tune the fit of the shelves to the notches. I scraped all of the parts and then hand-sanded them with #220-grit before assembly. The ends of the shelves slide into the notches and are simply glued and clamped.

It's a bit of a challenge to keep everything lined up during assembly. I started the shelves in the notches before brushing in glue.

To keep the shelves aligned while clamping, I placed ¾"-thick sticks on my bench to support the back edges.

This is the distance from the wall in the finished shelf. I also made sure that the ends of the back uprights were flat on the surface of the bench.

After a final hand sanding with #280-grit, I finished the shelves with three coats of lacquer sprayed from an aerosol can.

Curved parts aren't hard to make, and can be both structural and visually interesting. The ability to make them adds to the skills that make a well-rounded woodworker.

Use layout lines on the top of the bending form to attach guide strips for the router. Working from the center, I also established lines for the ends of the supports. Then I notched the curved parts for the shelves with the router

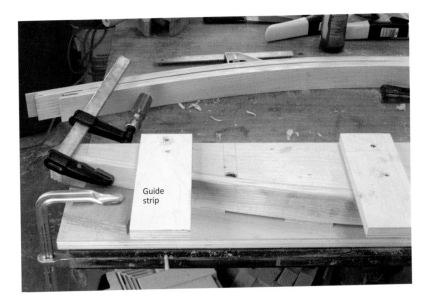

Guide strip

The other edge is ripped on the table saw, maintaining contact with the table on the infeed side of the saw blade.

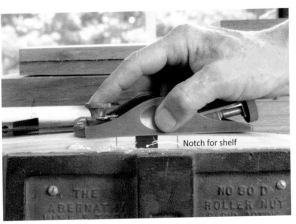

Notch for shelf

With the finished part back in the jig, I lay out a 2"-long flat at the center of each curved piece and then plane it by hand. Check the fit by measuring the space between the two parts at the shelf locations.

The ends of the shelves fit in the notches. Adjust the fit with a few swipes with a smoothing plane. Mark the support locations on the bottom of the shelves to keep the parts in line during assembly.

Hanging the Shelves

To hang the shelves, I made two small blocks to fit behind the top of the back uprights. The dimensions of the blocks aren't critical, but they need to fit neatly together, and be tight against the inside of the curved support. I started with blocks larger than I needed so that I could cut them to shape while keeping my fingers a safe distance from the band saw blade. After cutting the blocks to shape I fit the curved edge to the back of the shelf support.

These can be fastened to a wall with Zip-it anchors (available from your local home center) after drawing a level line on the wall. The matching half of the hanger is glued to the back of each of the curved uprights. To hang the shelf on the wall, it is simply dropped in place on the hangers.

Lay out the hanging blocks on a piece of wood big enough to let you cut them safely on the band saw.

Cut the curve first, then make two short cuts to form the interlocking joint. The last cut frees the hanger from the block.

The bottom half of the hanging cleat is attached to the wall forming a hook.

The other half of the hanger is glued to the back of the shelf support, letting the shelves hang nearly invisibly.

Line up the shelves in the notches, then brush glue on all surfaces of the joint.

Sticks to support shelves

Assemble the shelves on a flat surface, making sure the ends are flat on the table. Square sticks keep the backs of the shelves in position.

thirteen

Corner Shelf

by MEGAN FITZPATRICK

With this simple and casual storage unit you have a couple of options when it comes to stock selection. You might wish to make your own panels for the backs, top and shelf. But, you can also buy already glued-up panels of pine at the home center for just a little more cash outlay, so that's what I did for this project. My shopping trip for this corner shelf was quick and easy. I picked up two 24" × 48" pine panels, one pine 1" × 8" × 3' for the sides, one pine 1" × 2" × 2' for the rail, and two double hooks with a rubbed-nickel finish.

Start by cutting your top to the proper-sized square; the rest of the pieces simply need to fit under it, as shown. While the top in my version is 23½" square, you can easily makes yours smaller (or larger), and base the size of your other pieces off the top, calculating in a ¾" overhang.

To cut all the panels to size, I clamped a straightedge with a beefy edge to the piece, 1½" to the left of my cutline, and used that as a rail along which to guide the jigsaw. (Note that one back piece is 21¼" wide, the other is 22" wide because they overlap.) Depending on the width of your jigsaw (or circular saw) base, your setup may vary. To set your straightedge location, simply measure from the edge of the blade to the outside of your baseplate. That's the offset for your guide.

To join the two back pieces, lay the narrow back piece face down on a table, line up a thick caul (a piece of 2×4 works well) across the edge, and clamp it in place. This allows you a flat reference surface against which to balance the wide back piece as you drill holes and screw the pieces together (I used 1½" × #8 screws). Set the back pieces aside, and move on to the top and shelf.

To make the 45° cuts across the top and shelf, use the same jig setup as for the panels. On the top, the angle begins 8" from the back corners; on the shelf, it's at 6½".

The sides were simply chopped to 7¼" length from the dimensional stock to 16" at the miter saw.

Then, I measured in 1½" from the bottom edge, grabbed a handy bucket off our shop shelves, and used that to draw my arcs. The arc ended at 6" from the side's bottom edge, so that's where I installed the shelf later in the process. The position of your shelf can vary based on your radius – or based on what you think looks most attractive. There's no structural reason that the shelf be aligned with the curve.

Cut to size. Cutting your top to size first allows you to easily fit everything that goes under it, even if you change the dimensions to suit your specifications.

Straightedge jig. A straightedge with a beefy edge makes a good guide for making straight cuts with a jigsaw or circular saw.

What's on hand. You don't need a compass to draw an arc. Just grab whatever's handy around the house. I used a bucket with an 11" diameter to its outer rim.

After marking and cutting one side with a jigsaw, I used that cut to mark the second side. I then cut it, clamped the two together, and did the final shaping and smoothing with a rasp and #120-grit sandpaper. I also sanded to clean up saw cuts and break the edges.

Now it's time to put it all together. First, position your shelf and mark on the back of both back pieces the location for your screw holes (I used five screws across each back piece). Drill pilot holes at the marked locations into the positioned shelf, then sink your screws.

Position your side pieces with the top edge aligned with the top of the back pieces, and drill pilot holes and countersinks to attach the sides to both the backs and shelf (I used four screws along the side, and two to hold the sides tight to the shelf).

Nail (or screw) the top in place after drilling pilot holes, making sure you have an even overhang on both sides.

The last step is to measure across the front edge just under the top, and cut your rail to length. So that it fits snugly into the angled opening, cut 45° angles on both ends. Now run a bead of glue along the top edge, position it, drill pilot holes and nail it in place.

Now that everything is assembled, fill your screw and nail holes, then paint, add the hooks where you like them, and you're done.

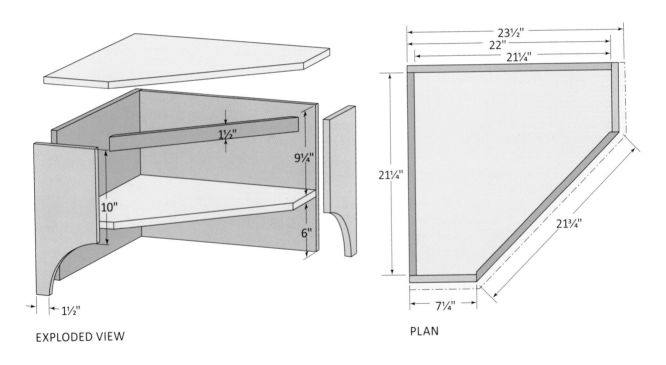

EXPLODED VIEW

PLAN

Corner Shelf

NO.	PART	INCHES			STOCK	MILLIMETERS			COMMENTS
		T	W	L		T	W	L	
1	Narrow back	¾	21¼	16	Pine	19	539	406	
1	Wide back	¾	22	16	Pine	19	559	406	
2	Sides	¾	7¼	16	Pine	19	184	406	
1	Top	¾	23½	23½	Pine	19	597	597	
1	Shelf	¾	21¼	21¼	Pine	19	539	539	
1	Top rail	¾	1½	21¾	Pine	19	38	552	45° on both ends

fourteen

Wine Rack

by DAVID THIEL

Once upon a time, I was a beer guy and I still enjoy a good brew. But recently I've also learned to appreciate a glass of good wine. Usually a bottle or two of red wine in the house is adequate, but as my interest in wine has grown, so has my interest in having a selection of wines available. So I decided I needed a wine rack.

I don't have a lot of room in my house, so I turned to my computer-aided design program. After carefully measuring a variety of bottles (between sips) I calculated the best way to maximize my bottle storage in the smallest amount of space. The rack shown here is my best effort, with storage for 24 bottles (two cases) in a 20" x 20" x 14"-deep space.

This design allows for an efficient cutting list and an efficient use of space. I was able to design the rack using 11 pieces of wood in only four sizes. Maybe that's why I decided to complicate it by adding dovetails to the solid mahogany box. That, and the need for reliable strength – 24 bottles of wine are heavy.

The interior dividers are eggcrate-joined Baltic birch with veneer tape applied to the front edges. Designed to hang on a wall with a hidden French cleat, the box could be easily adapted for floor use with a simple base and maybe a drawer added above the box itself. It's a reasonable weekend project with some time left over to have a glass of wine and appreciate your work.

Building the Cabinet

Start construction with the outside of the case. The four pieces are exactly the same, 14" x 20", but because this is a simple piece, an attractive grain pattern can go a long way to make it more dramatic. I was lucky to have a slab of mahogany tucked away in the shop that was actually 14½" wide, which allowed me to avoid any glued-up panels.

After choosing the most attractive faces of the boards for the exterior, start laying out the dovetails. Everyone has their own method of making dovetails, and you may choose to cut yours by hand to get a more unique spacing pattern. I chose the easy plugged-in route and used a model 2200 Keller Jig (kellerdovetail. com, $239) to cut through-dovetails.

Keep On Groovin'

With the dovetails cut and fit, you will need to cut grooves for the back in all four pieces. Because I was hanging my rack on the wall, I allowed a ¾" setback

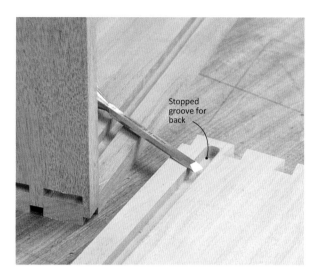

The box itself is dovetailed together. When laying out your dovetails, make sure the back groove falls between the tails and the pins on the sides so the groove won't show at the top. I had to run stopped-grooves on the sides to avoid the groove showing from the outside. All you have to do is stop the cut, then use a chisel to square out the end of the groove.

from the rear of each piece and used a ½" router bit in my router table to make the ⅜"-deep grooves.

With the spacing I used on my dovetails, the grooves in the top and bottom pieces are able to run the entire length of the piece without interfering with the dovetail pattern. However, on the side pieces I had to use a stopped groove to avoid seeing the groove in the assembled box.

After running the stopped grooves, use a chisel to square out the ends. Next dry-assemble the box with the back in place to make sure everything fits well.

An Interlocking Complexity

The divided interior of the box is formed from just six pieces of ½" plywood, notched to interlock with one another.

Start by measuring from one inside corner of the box to the opposite corner. While a measurement for the length of these pieces is provided here, it's a good idea to double-check the dimensions against your project.

Your dimensions for the two long dividers should be the same, but if they're not, cut the pieces to the required lengths, then use your table saw to bevel both sides of each end at 45° to form a point on each. Cut

To fit the interlocking dividers to one another, start with the two long dividers. First fit them between the corners of the box, then mark the overlapping locations of the two pieces. The eggcrate notches are cut at the mark. Follow this same process to fit and notch the four smaller dividers.

Veneer tape added to tighten fit

This photo (with the dividers removed from the box) gives a better example of how the dividers all fit together. If you look closely at the right edge of the piece being dropped into place, you'll see a trick I had to use to fix a "too-loose" divider. By adding veneer tape to the beveled end I was able to fix the fit. Veneer tape added to the front of the divider after the fix made the fix virtually invisible.

them a little long at first, then fit the pieces so they slide snugly into the case.

When the pieces fit, slide one all the way in, then slide the other in against the first. Mark both to indicate the intersecting spot, as shown in the photo at right.

Take the pieces out and use a try square and the intersection marks to lay out the 5" x ½" notches on each piece. Then head to the band saw and cut out the notches. Don't worry about being too neat, but cutting close to the inside of the lines allows for fine-tuning the fit. Test the two pieces in the case and move on to the last four dividers.

To locate the four smaller divider locations, start by marking the center line on each of the four sides. This mark is where the pieces will meet at 45° angles. Measure the necessary lengths of the four pieces (hope-

fully these lengths are the same) and then cut the four pieces to length, adding 45° bevels at all the ends.

Next, remove the front diagonal divider and fit two of the short dividers in place at the top left and bottom right corners of the rack, parallel with the remaining long divider. Place the front long divider back in its place, and again mark the notch locations on all the dividers.

The notches should be centered on the short dividers, but it's best to check the location against the actual pieces. Make your notches, then repeat the process with the short dividers for the bottom left and the top right corners. With everything fitting snugly in place, I added some birch veneer tape to the front edges of the dividers to hide the layered plywood.

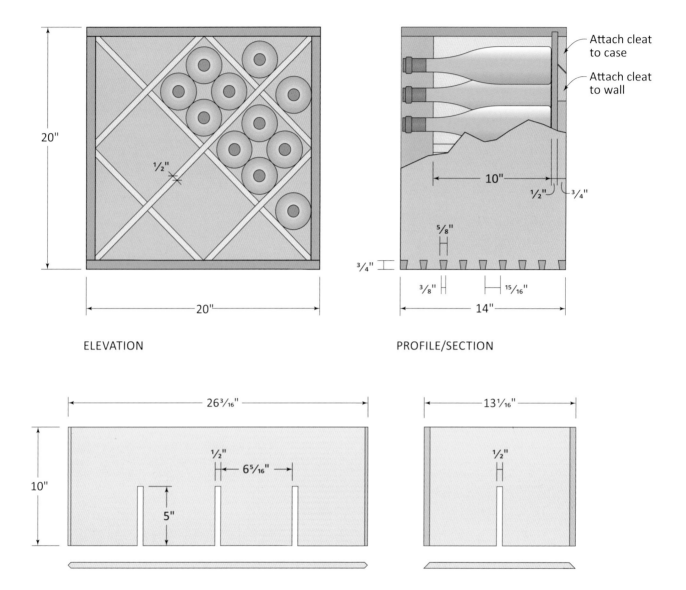

ELEVATION

PROFILE/SECTION

Attach cleat to case

Attach cleat to wall

LONG DIVIDER PLAN & SECTION

SHORT DIVIDER PLAN & SECTION

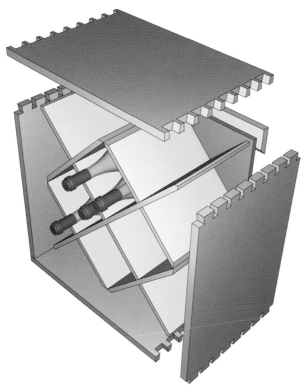

EXPLODED VIEW

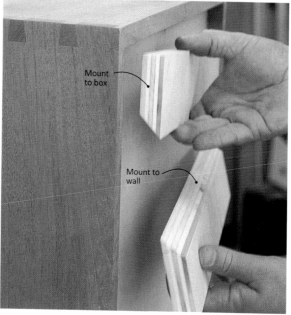

To hang the box on a wall I used a French cleat. The photo shows the two parts of the cleat pulled away from the recessed back of the box. Trés simple!

Color & Character

Before gluing up the case, decide how you're going to finish it. I opted to leave the birch plywood pieces natural, but I used Moser's water-soluble Light Sheraton Mahogany aniline dye (Woodworker's Supply, 800-645-9292 or woodworker.com, item #W13301, $11.99 for 1 oz.) on the mahogany box. Because the back is birch plywood, I'd have trouble dying the box after assembly without coloring the back, too.

My solution was to give the back a few coats of a clear lacquer finish prior to assembly. Then, when the dye is applied to the mahogany, any errant dye that gets on the back simply can be wiped off the lacquer finish.

After sanding the interior of the project, it's time to move on to the glue-up stage. Make sure the dovetails are pulled up tight and the case is square.

Measure from corner to corner in both directions and make any necessary adjustments.

After the glue is dry, take the case out of the clamps and flush up the pins and tails. This may require sanding or you may choose to use a sharp low-angle block plane to flush the sides.

Marrying the Rack to a Wall

To hang the rack, I used a French cleat. This is so simple I'm surprised it doesn't get used more often. The cleat is made by cutting a 5"-wide piece of ¾" plywood to fit between the two box sides. Then simply set your table saw blade to a 45° angle and rip the piece in half lengthwise.

By attaching the top half of the cleat (widest-width facing out) to the case and the lower half to your wall (use drywall anchors if that's not possible) you simply can slide the case down onto the wall cleat using the 45° angle and lock it tightly in place.

A Strong, Woody Finish

Remove the dividers one last time and finish the box as you see fit. A coat of clear lacquer on the dividers will protect against time (and unsightly red wine spills) and make it easier to slide the bottles in and out of the rack.

When the dividers are again reassembled in place, a couple of accurately placed nails through the back into the dividers will hold them firmly in place.

Seeing so many interesting opportunities for taste-bud titillation tastefully displayed in my house is almost as gratifying as the project itself.

fifteen

Shaker Oval Boxes

by JOHN WILSON

There was a time when households had few belongings, when clutter from too much stuff was not an issue. Basics such as matches, glue powders and paint pigments, and sugar, coffee, tea and spices needed containers. Before the age of canisters and Tupperware, the Shaker craftsmen made and marketed their oval boxes.

The place for boxes in the home has changed throughout time. Modern metal and plastic containers have displaced the traditional preeminence of wooden boxes in the pantry. Today they are more often seen on the coffee table in a more decorative setting. Along with the change in use has come a change in finish so that varnish rather than paint is preferred. Cherry is more common for bands than plain maple. Yet this is still a box for all occasions, utilitarian as well as decorative. Its charm and grace make a difference for whatever role it plays.

These beautiful boxes were first made from hard maple and white pine. In an age before machines, thin wood strips were rived from a straight billet of wood and made ready for bending by handplanes and scrapers. Hot water soaking makes this sturdy wood pliable, and bending gives a complete oval shape in a single motion. Tacked and made secure by oval shapers, this efficient process impresses me every time I do it.

The Search to Find Wood that Bends

Today we are not likely to go to the wood lot for a straight-grained section of log to split stock for the bands. Few of us have a wood lot nearby, and technology has separated us from skilled hand-tool use. But the need for bendable wood to flex around the box core remains the same. This capacity to flex is not always apparent in wood. While straight-grained stock is the place to begin to look for bending material, brittleness can cause the best looking piece to snap. One condition that causes brittleness is drying out. It's a consequence of the fact that we live some distance from the wood lot. Green wood, which bends best, isn't readily available.

In your search for materials for bending wood you will find hard maple a good species. Cherry, while it makes a fine box, is prone to changes in growth direction and unexpected brittleness. I sometimes imagine Shaker craftsmen watching my frustration with ornery cherry boards and sighing, "Ah, the price of vanity. Stick to the utility of maple, and it would go well."

Strange as it seems, the same things that make for suppleness in the human body (age and nutrition) apply

1. The table saw is my tool of choice for resawing bands up to 3" wide, although things slow down appreciably when nearing the capacity of the 10" blade. A sharp blade is a must. The zero-clearance wood insert shown here will prevent the thin wood from dropping through the table. When your setup is cutting effectively, there is little sanding required.

2. Resawing on the band saw can handle stock of 6" or more depending on the capacity of your machine. The resaw jig guides the cut. Clean up the board's sawn edge between each cut to give one smooth side. A drum sander gives a finished face to the sawn side. The blade shown is a ¼" Timber Wolf four-teeth-per-inch band that's used for general work in my shop. Others prefer a silicon-carbide hook-tooth ½" or ¾" blade.

to wood. Freshly cut boards do better than old dried ones. Also, the conditions of favorable growth will yield better results. Ample nutrients and sunlight make for faster growth as evidenced in wider annual rings. This is a favorable sign in selecting wood for bending. And, of course, straight growth, and not picturesque gnarled figure, is ideal.

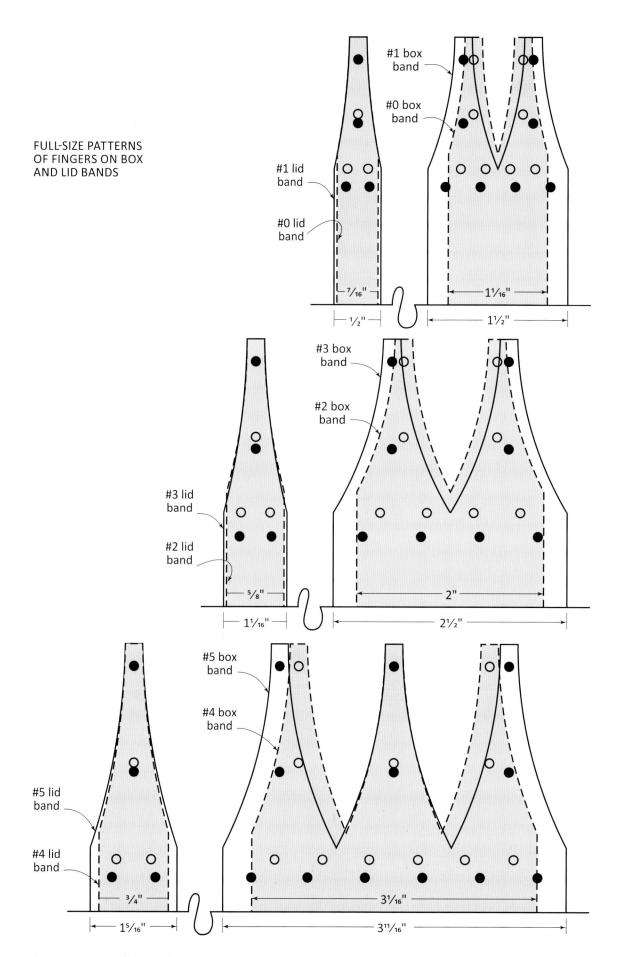

FULL-SIZE PATTERNS OF FINGERS ON BOX AND LID BANDS

#1 box band

#0 box band

#1 lid band

#0 lid band

7/16"

1/2"

1 1/16"

1 1/2"

#3 box band

#2 box band

#3 lid band

#2 lid band

5/8"

1 1/16"

2"

2 1/2"

#5 box band

#4 box band

#5 lid band

#4 lid band

3/4"

1 5/16"

3 1/16"

3 11/16"

Cutting Band Stock

Where will you find such wood for your box bands? The wood you use may be recently cut for firewood, or you may have luck with an old board of unknown species. The real test is to try it. Dimension a piece and slab off thin bands on your table saw or band saw. Photos 1 and 2 on page 93 show it being done. The table saw needs a zero-clearance insert to reduce the gap next to the blade to prevent the thin band from disappearing down the slot. Avoid short stock. Small box bands 12" to 20" long are cut more effectively and safely when sawn double length, 24" to 40" long. The blade is the key. I use thin-kerf 10" 40-tooth blades with alternate top-bevel design. Try a new blade to see what factory sharp can do.

When the table saw, blade and wood are in sync, the result is a finished band ready to use with little or no sanding.

The band saw needs a steady rest as a guide for thickness. A sharp blade is important here as well. I use a ¼" four-tooth-per-inch Timber Wolf. Others prefer a ½" or ¾" carbide-tipped blade for their band saw. A thicknessing drum sander will reliably finish the band to the specifications given in the table on page 103. The planer may not work well for thicknessing because of the thinness of the bands. They can catch in the blades and shatter. When planing just a few bands, try sticking them on a shooting board with double-stick tape to stiffen them.

However you cut your wood, be patient and be prepared to try again. You can get a feel for flexibility in the wood as it comes off the saw. I heat my shop with what doesn't work.

Sliced Veneer Stock

Veneer is another source for bands. This is wood dimensioned by slicing at a veneer mill. It is an efficient use of the best grade of logs as there is no saw kerf waste. Successive sheets of uniform thickness make it attractive. Great quantities are sliced for the furniture trade for high-quality face veneers.

Most of this is cut to ¼2" (.024") thickness making it too thin for our use in boxes. The other common thickness is ¹⁄₁₆", which works for smaller boxes, and you can expect reasonable bending results from hard maple. (One commercial source is Constantines: 954-561-1716 or constantines.com.)

When the log is sliced, the knife leaves one side of the veneer with slight crack lines. This "open side" face needs to be inside the box when bent. Otherwise, the surface will be rough and could splinter. Gently flexing the veneer prior to preparation for soaking may reveal a side with these slight crack lines. Placing it in water will always show this. What happens is the wood takes a slight curl across the grain when wet. The rule is this: The inside of the curl is the outside of the box.

I have built my business during the past 20 years on meeting the needs of the oval box trade (ShakerOvalBox.com). I use veneered band stock selected and dimensioned specifically for bending. While I welcome your business, I know that cutting bands in the manner described above can be both rewarding and of high quality. For instance, there is no bias side in sawn band stock. Many of you have the capacity to do your own cutting. It is worth the effort. Try widths of 2" and narrower that cut easily on the table saw. Wider stock has been known to be more difficult.

Top & Bottom Boards

The other materials needed for box making are the oval boards for the top and bottom. These are ¼" to ⁷⁄₃₂" thick and not bent. Unlike the stock for the bands, these are readily available. The oval shape sets off some interesting figures and features. It is an opportunity to use small sections of boards that accumulate from other work.

The one factor you need to consider in tops and bottoms is wood expansion. If the oval board expands too much in humid weather, the band will crack. Breakage is serious stuff, and is ever present in a box. The larger the box size, the more likely it is to occur. The reverse of this is the board drying out after you make your box. That will result in gaps where it meets the band, spoiling your nice tight fit. Where possible you want quartersawn stock to minimize the future effects of humidity change.

One solution to wood movement in larger box sizes is to use plywood. The cross banding of alternative plys stabilizes the wood. For appearance sake, pick plywood without a joint in the veneer face, and be careful not to sand through the very thin face veneers.

It is also a fact that different tree species expand and contract differently. Softwoods are more stable than hardwoods. The Shakers used quartersawn eastern white pine because it is a very stable cut of wood. You can find a table listing wood behavior as moisture changes in R. Bruce Hoadley's "Understanding Wood" (Taunton). Based on variation in species movement, I

3. Profile the finger design to rough dimension before final trimming with a utility knife. The locations for copper tacks are drilled at this time, too.

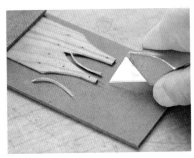

4. My preference for trimming is a utility knife with a fixed, not retractable, blade. This gives the necessary control. Use heavy-duty blades, not the lighter ones that come with a new knife.

5. The inside end of a band is feathered back 1" to 1½" depending on its thickness. This will provide a fair curve to the inside of the box.

opt for plywood when maple tops and bottoms reach 7" wide, cherry at 8" wide and pine at 12" wide.

Whatever your species and growth orientation, be sure the moisture content of the tops and bottoms are similar to the inside environment of your home. If you are uncertain of that, and do not own a moisture meter, never fear. Boards ¼" thick will adjust to your home's humidity level in a few days. Bring the top and bottom boards inside before you make your box and expose all the surfaces equally for a few days to allow this to happen.

Setting Up Your Bench
To dimension bending stock and top and bottom boards takes the resources of a full shop. Many craftsmen choose to purchase dimensioned materials and thus simplify their operation. The equipment and shop space to do the actual box making is quite modest. Even those without access to a wood shop can do it.

I always have used a combination of hand and power tools. Standard floor-model sized machines are fine, but smaller ones work well. A 10" band saw and a 4" x 36" belt sander with 6" disc, both benchtop machines, are suited to box making. An electric drill rounds out the power equipment. If you wish to do the cutting, shaping and drilling all by hand, that should not be too much of a challenge either. After all, original boxes predate these modern conveniences.

To set up your shop for this project you need a few jigs that are easy to make or find. You need a tray for soaking the bands. Normally, it needs to be long enough to fully immerse the largest size, 32" for the #5 box.

However, alternating ends for soaking can allow you to get by with something shorter. Box makers traditionally use hot water for this process. The alternatives to hot water are cool water and steam. All three methods work, but there are some differences in technique that go with each.

If you are already set up for steam bending, then by all means use it. If you can obtain a metal tray at least 4" x 32", then you are ideally set for hot water soaking. Set the tray on a stove or electric hot plate with stabilizer blocks under each end (photo 7). A length of steel gutter (the modern flat-bottom style) with end caps attached together with a ¾" plywood cover will serve for this.

When hot water is used, soaking takes 15 minutes. The wrap itself goes quickly with a few motions around the core.

Cool water will be the option when neither of the above is available, as you can co-opt the bathtub. Understand that flexibility comes from both soaking and heat, and when only one condition is involved, as in cool water, soaking you must allow 12 to 24 hours of soaking and use more finesse when bending. A forward then back motion to bending in small increments as you go around the tight end of the oval will flex the wood under circumstances such as this.

When tacking the lap, you will need an anvil for clinching the points of the tacks. This can be made from an 8" length of 1" or 1¼" galvanized pipe bolted to a wood cradle and clamped to your bench (photo 9).

Cores & Shapers
In addition to a soaking tray you need a set of cores and a set of shapers. The core is a wood plug the size of the inside of a box. The hot, wet band is bent around it (photo 8). Made from soft wood (2" foam board also can be used), they are created using the oval patterns at right.

The shapers are the key to the Shakers' box production (photo 10). You will need a pair for each box made at one soaking. If you wish to make five of one sized box, then 10 shapers are needed. The alternative is to bend on five successive occasions, which is a lot more work than making a few extra shapers. They are made to the same oval pattern as the cores, only they have a 10° beveled edge to act as corks in the oval opening. Cut them slightly oversized by cutting ¹⁄₁₆" outside your pattern line. Drill holes for ventilation and to allow you to grab them for removal after the band is dry. The wood for shapers can be solid or ply, and the thickness varies. The smallest ellipse is ½" thick, mid-sized is ⅝" thick, and sizes #5 and larger use ¾" stock.

Preparing the Box Band

Now you can begin the box-making process. Cut and drill the bands for the fingers. Photo 3 shows the band marked according to the finger pattern for shape and location of the tack holes. The locations of the copper tacks are drilled with a ³⁄₆₄" or ¹⁄₁₆" bit. The swallow tails, as the Shakers sometimes referred to the fingers, are cut on a band saw, or this can be accomplished completely with a knife. The rough shape is trimmed (photo 4) to the graceful proportions of the finished box. There are three elements to this shape: narrow width, slight bevel to the edges and a curved, gothic shape. I mention these because almost everyone starts by making the fingertips too blunt and too beveled – losing the graceful curve of the pattern in the process of trimming. The fingertip needs to be only slightly wider than the diameter for the copper tack head. This will make wrapping, tacking and drying go well, and achieve a more Shaker look. The beveled edges are trimmed to a slight 10°, not approaching the 45° commonly cut by novices.

Now you should feather back the inside end of the band 1" to 1½" depending on the thickness of the band stock (photo 5). The sander with a block of wood to hold the veneer evenly is used to taper the end (photo 6).

When the band is trimmed and feathered, place it in hot water to soak (photo 7). Water hotter than 180° Fahrenheit will soften the lignin in the wood fiber that allows it to be bent. Upon drying it will hold the

6. The 4" x 36" bench sander sees a lot of use when I make a nesting set of five boxes. Here feathering the end of the band is controlled by a wood block to ensure a gradual taper.

Hot plate

Stabilizer block

7. The band has been feathered on one end and the fingers are trimmed and drilled on the other. The hot water tray has an electric hot plate with wood blocks under each end for stability. While a full boil is not necessary, water more than 180° will effect a softening of the lignin.

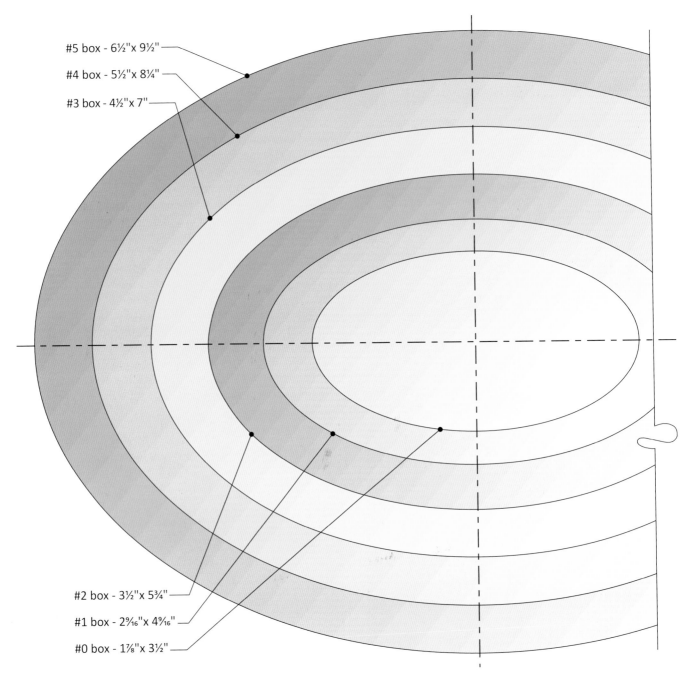

#5 box - 6½"x 9½"

#4 box - 5½"x 8¼"

#3 box - 4½"x 7"

#2 box - 3½"x 5¾"

#1 box - 2⁹⁄₁₆"x 4⁹⁄₁₆"

#0 box - 1⅞"x 3½"

OVAL PATTERNS FOR CORES AND SHAPERS

new shape. Soaking for 15 minutes is sufficient for ordinary bands. However, double that time for very small box sizes with a tight curve, and for troublesome bending stock.

Bending the Oval Band

Your soaked band will cool quickly once it is taken from the tray. When this operation goes in a smooth even motion, band breakage is minimized. Your core will

need a pencil mark to show where to start the feathered end of the band in bending. This is how you find that mark: The major tack line is centered in the front of the oval. The start mark is left of center. How far left? It's the same distance as the measurement between the main tack line and the tips of the fingers.

Copper tacks clinch the band. No glue is needed for this efficient fastening. The tacks are ¹⁄₁₆" longer than two layers of veneer. So two or three sizes of tacks are

8. The wet band is wrapped around a core the size of the inside of the box. Here the wrapped band is being given a pencil mark so that the core can be removed and the band returned to its proper size. Note that both fingers are held to prevent splitting between them. The mismatch at the lapped edges of the band is common at this stage and will be made even when tacking.

Fixing Mistakes

You might find two kinds of repairs helpful in your work. each using their own kind of glue. Wet bands that split can be repaired with cyanoacrylate (like Hot Stuff Original) two-part glue because it works on wet wood. The advantage of this is that any repair will hold the pliable wood before it dries. Minor gaps found around the edges of the oval board can be repaired with carpenter's glue. Wipe glue into the gap and sand immediately. The sander dust loads the wet glue, giving a matching glue line. Unlike cyanoacrylate that remains clear under varnish, carpenter's glue must be removed from the surface before finishing.

9. Small copper tacks ¹⁄₁₆" longer than the two thicknesses of veneer are used to clinch the lap. No glue is used. The wood cradle secures the pipe anvil to the bench.

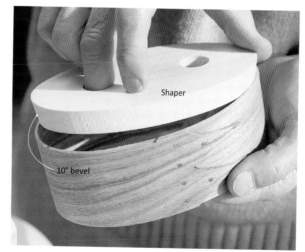

10. Once tacked, wood corks called shapers are put in both sides to hold the box shape for one to two days of drying. The 10° edge bevel and the holes for ventilation are a hallmark of this piece of bench equipment that is key to the Shaker system of production.

used for a set of boxes, which has thicker veneer for the larger sizes. Have your tacks, anvil, hammer, a pair of shapers and a core ready when the band is taken from the hot water.

The central operation of all box construction takes but a few seconds. In one smooth sweep, hold the feathered end at the start mark and bend halfway around. Change hands, hold and complete the wrap. Pencil a mark across the veneer lap to register the circumfer-

ence. Photo 8 shows this step completed. Hold both fingers securely at all times to avoid splitting the wood between them. Do not worry about having the edges exactly even or the main tack line centered at this stage. Both of these come next.

Open the band slightly to remove the core. Bring the band together so the pencil marks meet. Here is where you align the edges of the lapping band. Then tack the lap (photo 9).

11. The top band is wrapped on the box itself. It will be tacked and then returned to the box for drying. Note that the direction of the fingers match the bottom band fingers.

12. The construction of an oval box is half completed when it is set aside to dry for one to two days.

13. Here I'm tracing the oval on the ¼" boards used for tops and bottoms. A mechanical pencil will ensure accuracy of this line.

14. The disc sander finishes the edge up to the pattern line. The sander table is elevated to 4° to provide a slight cork effect to this ellipse for a tight fit. To make this adjustment, you may need to file out the slide slot so it no longer stops at 0°, or you can remove the thumb screw and use a small C-clamp.

15. The oval board is fitted into the bottom by setting it against the front lap and then working the back into place. This will ensure that the feathered end will not be damaged in the process of pushing the oval.

The last step is to place a shaper in both sides of the oval band. These can be rotated if needed to bring the main tack line into the center of the oval. The band is pliable while wet, so you can rotate the shaper. Match the second shaper with the position of the first to avoid a skewed band. Be gentle inserting the shaper and do not push too hard because this will flare the edges of the bands.

The lid band, which went in to soak along with the bottom band, is next. It is bent on the box itself, which acts as the core (photo 11). Size, alignment and centering are observed for this band as well. When tacked, the lid band goes in place with the fingers pointing the same way as the bottom fingers (photo 12). The first half of box construction will be complete when these two bands have thoroughly dried. Allow for normal air flow around the box. Avoid using extra heat, direct sun or fan blowing. Drying too quickly can result in the veneer warping.

Fitting Tops & Bottoms

The oval boards to complete the box are ¼" thick for mid-sized boxes, and ³⁄₁₆" and ⁷⁄₃₂" for the two smallest boxes.

Draw the oval by using the dry box band as the pattern. Remove the shapers and give the inside a light sanding. Use a mechanical pencil for an accurate line around the inside of the oval band. Now determine the direction of the fingers. It's up to you. Historically most boxes were pointing right, but significant numbers were lefties. In either case, both top and bottom bands should match.

Getting the top band finger direction to match that of the bottom band can be troublesome. The reason is this: When the lid is lying on the bench to be traced out, it is in the opposite position from where it is in place on the box. Check it out in position on the box to make sure that you have the right finger direction to match the bottom.

After band sawing the oval, sand the board up to the line on the disc sander (photo 14). This is not a right angle, but it has a slight bevel to give it a cork effect. To get this, adjust the disc table up 4°. Most sanding machines aren't designed to do this out of the box, but you can easily file the slide that adjusts the table to allow it to tip up the 4°.

Insert the oval board against the front edge first (photo 15), then press in the back. This avoids catching the feathered end of the band, which can be damaged. Press the board into the oval band until it is even or slightly below the band all the way around. Sand this joint line flush. Now repeat these steps for the lid section.

Wood Pegs Hold the Boards

Once the oval boards are in place and the joints sanded flush, it is time to drill for wood pegs. These holes center on the ¼" top and bottom boards, and are placed 2" to 3" apart around the edge. They keep the oval boards in place. It takes a ¹⁄₁₆" or ⁵⁄₆₄" hole drilled ½" deep. Two jigs are shown for ensuring that you do not miss the edge of the boards.

Photo 16 shows a small drill held down with a wood yoke to create a horizontal drilling jig. Photo 17 shows an adaptation for a drill press using a right angle clamped to the work surface. It drills in the vertical mode.

16. After the oval board is in place and sanded flush, drill the perimeter every 2" to 3" for wood pegs. This drill jig locks a spare drill to a board with a front table the right height to center the hole on the ¼" board inside.

17. An alternative drilling method makes use of a drill press. The jig, which I call a bookend, creates a vertical drilling station.

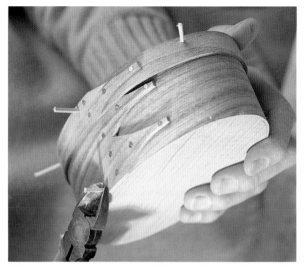

18. Wood pegs are made from cutting in half the box of World's Fair Brand toothpicks. The tapered end to these match the 5/64" hole for a secure fit when tapped in place.

19. Final sanding is done with a #120-grit belt replacing the #80-grit one used for shaping wood before.

The wood pegs can be split off a thin cutting of wood. However, in my shop, hardwood toothpicks made by the World's Fair Brand Co. serve for pegs. Cut the box in half on the band saw to double your count of pieces at just the right length. Tap the pegs in securely (no glue needed), and snip off with wire cutters (photo 18).

With the pegs in place, sand the surfaces of the box (photo 19). The finger lap is one area I do by hand to ensure that the curved finger design retains its full relief.

Finishing the Oval Box: Paint vs. Varnish

Boxes need a finish coat on the outside for protection, but remain plain wood on the inside. The reason for this is the neutral nature of wood. Just like the insides of bureau drawers, you do not want the odors from oil or paint finishes to affect food or cloth.

Historically, boxes were painted before the mid-1800s and clear finished after that. Paint was made locally from lime, clay, milk and pigments. Recipes for finishes were a shop tradition. Interestingly, craftsmen of old did not remove the lid when painting the box, so original boxes show a narrow band of plain wood around the top edge. This may be due to the possibility of a lid sticking to the homemade paint.

What do I recommend? First, if you do paint, take the lid off and save yourself the trouble of having to explain "incomplete" outside painting. Second, leave the inside plain. Third, use whatever finish you like, have on hand and are familiar with. There is nothing that is all that special about a box finish that should keep you from getting it done.

The little #1 box with red paint (shown on the cover) was finished with one coat of latex flat paint, followed by sanding with #220-grit sandpaper. This will accent the edges of the oval and finger area, and reveal the copper tacks. The new paint is finished with Kiwi brown shoe polish! That's right, I call it old-time patina in a can. Rub it on and brush it off. Note of caution: Try a sample of whatever wax finish you use before doing the box to ensure that the solvents in your wax do not "pucker" the surface of the paint.

Clear finishes come in a variety of forms such as shellac, varnish, lacquer, oil and blends of several of these. Some are brushed, some wiped on. Each has fans. All work. Your choice. For myself, I prefer quick-dry polyurethane for durability in areas where water spatter is likely, such as in the kitchen. This can be brushed on from the can, or mixed 50/50 with painter's naptha (a form of paint thinner) to make a wipe-on finish that avoids the nasty habit of varnishes getting runs or drips. Sand between coats.

Conclude with a rub on a brown paper sack. This is an old painter's trick that has been known to really work – simple, available, quick and effective. Open a paper grocery sack so the inside is lying flat open. You want to avoid rubbing on the ink printing on the outside lest it transfer to your fine finish. I have a piece of ¼" foam (used for carpet underlayment) under the paper to avoid encounters with grit on the bench that pokes through the paper. Then rub the top, bottom and sides. It takes less time to do it than reading about it, and it gives your box a smooth, burnished feel.

Sign and Date Your Creation

When the finish is done, you want to sign and date your handiwork. Did the Shakers sign their boxes? Yes and no. There was a feeling at times that the community was paramount and individual expressions of ownership inappropriate.

But there are many examples of boxes that were signed, and many of these were given as gifts, just like yours may be. I think it is a nice touch in this age of mass production to have your individual creation labeled with your own signature and date.

Having finished your first box project, be aware that you will receive both compliments and longing eyes directed to the oval boxes. There is no project in my experience that has such universal appeal as a Shaker oval box. Watch out, you may find yourself joining the ranks of box makers!

20. In this industrial age, craft work is highly valued. Sign your box with pride.

Shaker Oval Box Specifications

BOX SIZE	COPPER TACK SIZE	BAND THICKNESS	BOTTOM BAND WIDTH X LENGTH	TOP BAND WIDTH X LENGTH	ELLIPSE WIDTH X LENGTH	TOP & BOTTOM THICKNESS	NO. OF FINGERS & LENGTH TO TACK LINE
	*NOTES 1 & 2	*NOTE 3					
0	1	.062"	1¹⁄₁₆" x 11⅞"	⁷⁄₁₆" x 12¼"	1⅞" x 3½"	.195 - .210"	2 - 1⅜"
1	1	.065"	1½" x 15"	½" x 15½"	2⁹⁄₁₆" x 4⁹⁄₁₆"	.210 - .220"	2 - 1⁹⁄₁₆"
2	1½	.070"	2" x 19"	⅝" x 19¾"	3½" x 5¾"	.235 - .250"	2 - 1¹³⁄₁₆"
3	1½	.075"	2½" x 23"	¹¹⁄₁₆" x 24"	4½" x 7"	¼"	2 or 3 - 2¹⁄₁₆"
4	2	.080"	3¹⁄₁₆" x 27"	¾" x 28"	5½" x 8¼"	¼"	3 - 2¼"
5	2	.085"	3¹¹⁄₁₆" x 31"	¹⁵⁄₁₆" x 32"	6½" x 9½"	¼" - ⁵⁄₁₆"	3 - 2⁷⁄₁₆"

*NOTES: (1) Leave ¹⁄₁₆" exposed end of tack inside, tap to clinch. The #1 tack = ³⁄₁₆" long, #1½ = ⁷⁄₃₂" long, #2 = ¼" long. (2) Use ³⁄₆₄" or ¹⁄₁₆" pilot hole for #1, #1½ and #2 copper tacks. (3) Band thickness is in thousandths because these small differences are impossible to read with a tape measure and a difference of as little as .006" will change the wood's bending properties; larger changes (.015") can require you to use longer tacks. Purchase an inexpensive steel dial caliper (Grizzly sells a 4" caliper for $17.95; item# G9808; call 800-523-4777 or visit grizzly.com to order).

Silverware Tray

by CHRISTOPHER SCHWARZ

sixteen

Trying something new in the shop can be, well, trying. Once I get comfortable with one technique to make a joint, I am loathe to try another, no matter how many people (or magazines) tell me how much better it is.

This is human nature, I suppose. Whenever I want to attempt something new, I try to use it in a project that doesn't consume a lot of wood or time. That way, if I botch the project, I've made just a few sticks of firewood.

This Shaker silverware tray is an ideal project for this sort of experiment. Beginning dovetailers will find this project a good starter project. Want to try using rasps and files? The curves on the end pieces and the cutout handles are excellent practice. How about cutting rabbets or grooves with hand tools? Or even just hand-planing all the boards and giving your sander a rest? This article and its drawings explain how the box goes together; the methods you choose to execute those joints are up to you.

About the Box

All the parts for this project are ½"-thick stock. Using thin stock is what makes this project ideal for people who want to hone their dovetail skills. Thin stock is easier to cut true than thick stock. Cut all your parts to size and then cut your dovetails at all four corners.

The bottom of the tray is a single panel that floats in a groove cut into the sides and ends. The groove is ¼" x ¼". Cut the groove so it is located ⅝" up from the bottom edge of your sides and ends. Note that the groove in the two side pieces needs to be stopped or you will be able to see it on the outside of the project. The groove in the end pieces does not need to be stopped as its exit point will be hidden by the tails on your side pieces.

The bottom itself needs a tongue on all of its four edges so it will fit into the ¼" x ¼" groove. To create this tongue, cut a ½"-wide x ¼"-deep rabbet on all four edges of the bottom piece. The rabbet is wider than you need, but the extra width makes it easier to fit the bottom in the groove, and to get the bottom in and out of the groove during both test-fitting and assembly.

The size of the bottom piece is critical. It should bottom out in the groove in the end pieces. But the long edges of the bottom piece should have some room to allow the bottom to expand and contract with the change of seasons. The size of the bottom in the cutting list allows ¹⁄₁₆" for expansion on either side.

"New" way to make rabbets. A small-scale project such as this is a great way to try out different ways of making joints. Here I'm making the rabbet in the bottom with a moving fillister plane.

Cut the curves on the end pieces. The easiest way to mark the curve is to mark a line 1½" in from the top edge of the ends. Take a thin and long piece of scrap and bend it so it joins your two pencil marks on the ends and the top of the end. Trace the curve and cut it.

The cutout handles on the ends are ¾" high, 3" long and located ⅝" from the top edge of the end. Here's a hint: Use a ¾" auger or Forstner bit to both remove the waste and form the curves on the ends. Then refine and smooth the inside edges of each cutout.

Assemble the box by gluing two end pieces to one side piece. Then slide the bottom into its groove and glue the other side in place. My finish recipe for the box shown here is simple: Rag on a coat of boiled linseed oil (follow the instructions on the container) and allow the oil to fully cure. This takes a couple weeks in a warm room. Then spray on three coats of a clear aerosol lacquer, sanding lightly between each coat with #320-grit sandpaper.

You might be wondering what new technique I tried out when building this project. My new technique was to attempt to build this project for my wife for her January birthday and to actually deliver it on time. And how did I do? Let's just say it was an excellent Groundhog Day gift.

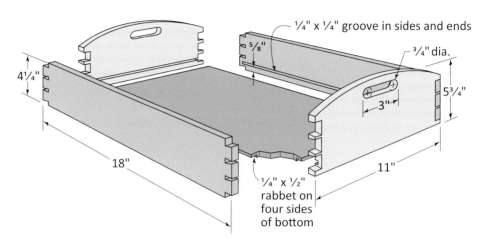

¼" x ¼" groove in sides and ends

5/8"

¾" dia.

4¼"

5¾"

3"

18"

11"

¼" x ½" rabbet on four sides of bottom

EXPLODED VIEW

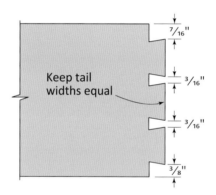

7/16"

Keep tail widths equal

3/16"

3/16"

3/8"

DOVETAIL LAYOUT

Silverware Tray

NO.	ITEM	DIMENSIONS (INCHES)			MATERIAL
		T	W	L	
2	Sides	½	4¼	18	Cherry
2	Ends	½	5¾	11	Cherry
1	Bottom	½	10⅜	17½	Cherry

Japanese Sliding-lid Box

by CHRISTOPHER SCHWARZ

While picking though a table of vintage Japanese tools for sale in 2013, I spotted this sliding-lid box under the vendor's table; it was blackened by age, soot and rust. Despite its scars, however, the box was still graceful and functional.

The owner, a Japanese carpenter, wouldn't part with it. But he let me measure and photograph the piece both inside and out so I could make a respectable version for myself.

The carpenter said it was a toolbox, and it would indeed fit a small kit of tools. But other experts in Japanese furniture said it was more likely a generic storage box that could be used to hold anything – wooden Tupperware, if you will.

The original was made using Douglas fir. For this article I made versions in both vertical-grain fir and Port Orford cedar, another wood preferred by Japanese joiners. The biggest challenge of the project was finding the dome-head nails. I settled on using No. 5 dome-head tacks (called "taiko byo") for Japanese drum making, though upholstery tacks with a head ½" diameter or smaller are a more economical choice. (Both choices are listed in the "Supplies" box.)

Construction is simple, yet achieving perfection is difficult thanks to all the small details. The corners of the box are joined by finger joints. Everything is reinforced by the dome-head nails.

Finger Joints

The finger joints at the corners of the carcase are quite large. This makes the layout simple, but the execution a challenge. I first laid out and cut the single socket on the side pieces, then transferred that shape to the ends to cut the single pin.

Don't forget that the sockets are ⅝" deep in ½"-thick material. This creates an ⅛" overlap at the box's corners and creates nice shadow lines.

After sawing the socket on the side pieces, remove the waste between with a coping saw and a chisel.

After sawing all the sockets, transfer their shapes to the end pieces to cut the single pin on the end of each end piece. To ensure the baseline of the side pieces is mated perfectly with the ends, tack a wooden ruler to the baseline of each side piece. This makes the transfer process foolproof.

Cutting the single pin on the end pieces is a chisel challenge. Saw and cope the waste. Then use a chisel to level the end grain. A square and a little patience will pay off.

Make the socket. Hand-cut finger joints are more demanding than dovetails. To ensure you are sawing square and plumb, first make several warm-up kerfs in the waste area before sawing the walls of the socket.

A quick sweep. A coping saw will quickly remove the waste in the socket. Then chop and pare the remaining waste away with a chisel.

No measuring. No matter how good a sawyer you are, every corner joint will be different. Transfer the shape of each socket onto its mating end piece using a knife.

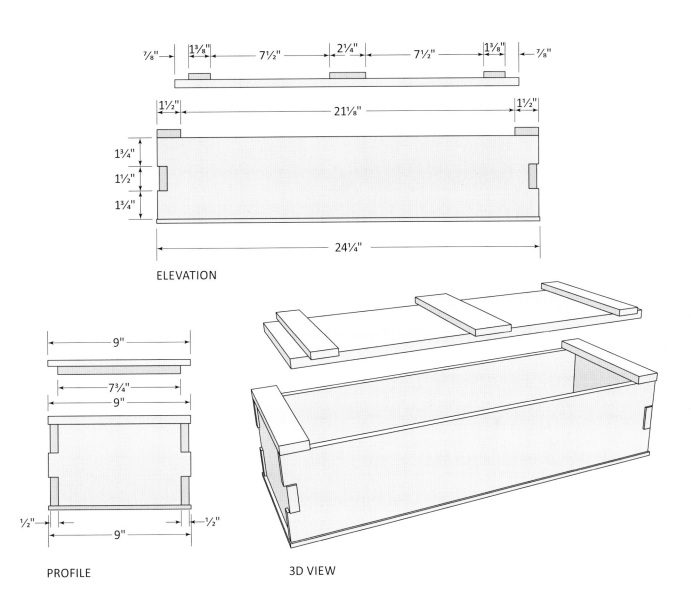

ELEVATION

PROFILE

3D VIEW

Japanese Sliding-lid Box

NO.	ITEM	DIMENSIONS (INCHES)			MATERIAL
		T	W	L	
2	Sides	½	5	24⅛	Port Orford cedar
2	Ends	½	5	9	Port Orford cedar
1	Bottom	¼	9	24¼	Port Orford cedar
1	Lid	½	7¾	21¾	Port Orford cedar
2	Small lid battens	½	1⅜	9	Port Orford cedar
1	Large lid batten	½	2¼	9	Port Orford cedar
2	Case battens	½	1½	9	Port Orford cedar

Flat & square. Work to the baseline with a chisel. Take light cuts and confirm the end grain is flat and square to the faces using a square.

Tape & clamp. Painter's tape protects your planed surfaces from glue. Clamps press the corners tight.

Now fit the joints together. If you have never cut finger joints by hand before, read this next sentence with care: Hand-cut finger joints have to be assembled like dovetail joints.

What does that mean? You can't just hammer the end pieces down into the side pieces. Unless your sawing was perfect – 90° in all directions – they won't go together easily, or at all. Instead, slide the end pieces into the side piece sockets to pull up "one way." This might sound confusing until you cut the joint. But it's really no different than realizing that the tailboard and pinboard of a dovetail joint go together in only one way.

The last bit of work before assembly is to chisel a ¹⁄₁₆" x ¹⁄₁₆" chamfer on the corners of the finger joints. Lay out the chamfers in pencil, then use a chisel to remove the pencil lines.

Assemble the Carcase

The original box was unfinished – its surfaces were left straight from the plane. Even if you want to apply finish to your box, the overlapping joints at the corners will make cleaning up glue squeeze-out difficult.

So the best thing to do is tape off the joints so that glue squeeze-out will end up on the tape. This takes only about 10 minutes and makes a world of difference.

Also, I use liquid hide glue, so clean-up is easy, even if the clamps prevent you from scouring every nook and cranny. After the clamps are off, a little hot water and a toothbrush can remove remaining bits of glue.

After the glue has cured, remove the clamps and the tape, then add the dome-head nails. The drum nails have a thin shank that is square in section. While you could drive these in without a pilot hole, I prefer to bore a ¹⁄₁₆"-diameter pilot hole for each nail to prevent its shaft from wandering.

As you can see from the photos below, the nails on the side pieces are not centered; they are "cheated" a

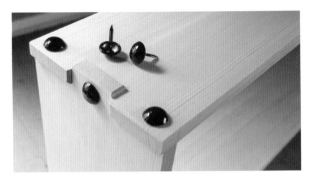

Decorative security. These dome-head nails don't hold as well as a cut nail, but they do add strength and prevent the wood from getting scuffed.

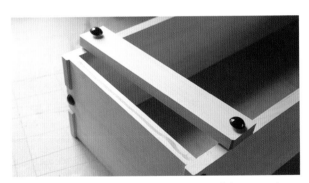

Here's the point. To prevent the battens from sliding around, drive the dome-head nails into each batten so the tips protrude just a bit. Add the glue. Then press the batten in place. The tips of the nails will prevent the batten from sliding.

bit toward the top and bottom to add holding power to the joint. Drill each pilot hole ½" in from the long end of each side piece. The nails through the end pieces are centered on the pin.

Now add the battens to the case that will capture the lid. These battens are glued and nailed to the ends.

Look close. The 2d brads are angled just a bit to add some wedging action. This keeps the bottom on through years of service.

Reinforcements. The screws ensure the battens won't come loose years from now. My stock is perfectly quartersawn, so there isn't much of a concern with wood movement. If your lid will move a lot, you might want to ream out the screws' clearance holes in the lid to allow for movement.

Add the Bottom

The bottom of the box is thin, nailed on and overhangs the assembled carcase just a tad. Plane up the bottom piece, then attach it to the carcase with 2d headed nails (1" long). I used cut brads. Again, a ¹⁄₁₆" pilot hole is good insurance to prevent the nails from wandering.

The other detail about these brads is that each one is angled a bit – about 7° – to wedge the bottom on the carcase. This is sometimes called "dovetailing" your nails.

After driving the brads in, set the heads ¹⁄₃₂" below the surface to prevent the heads from scratching up a nicely finished tabletop.

Make the Lid

The lid slides and locks thanks to the battens that are fastened to the lid and the carcase. The dome-head nails alone do not offer enough holding power, so the three lid battens also are screwed to the lid.

I used ⅞" #4 roundhead screws to attach the battens from the inside of the lid. I chose roundhead screws because their heads' shape mimicked the shape of the dome-head nails.

Screw the lid to the battens – two screws per batten – then flip the lid over and add the dome-head nails. Note that the dome-head nails are located a bit more toward the center of the lid than the remainder of the nails on the box. I put them 1½" from the ends of each batten.

Add the pull to one end of the carcase and the box is complete. I left my boxes unfinished, though you could add a coat of wax to the exterior to give it some protection.

While the boxes look nice and crisp now, I look forward to seeing them in 20 years when their scars will make them look even better.

supplies

kaDON
kadon.com

#5 Taiko byo (tacks)
$115/1,000

Van Dyke's Restorers
vandykes.com or 800-237-8833

Burnished brass tacks
#02362511, $7.99/100

Shiny nickel tacks
#225060, $10.99/100

Tremont Nail Co.
tremontnail.com or 800-835-0121

2d Standard brad
#CRB2, $23.47/1 lb. box

Lee Valley
leevalley.com or 800-871-8158

Tansu steel handles
#00D55.50, $7 ea.

Prices correct at time of publication.

Gifts & Decor

eighteen

Outdoor Lantern

by CHRISTOPHER SCHWARZ

Call me dull, but I've never been a Tiki torch kind of guy. And the last time we lit an outdoor party we used oil lamps – which, because of the flammable nature of oil, almost ended in disaster. So my task before our next party was to build a lantern that's low-key and electric (to ensure that only ribs were barbecued and not the neighbor's dog).

This lamp can be used in a variety of ways. It looks great on a patio table, or you could glue 6"-long dowels into the feet and stake it in your garden. Either way, it's going to stand up to the elements.

The lantern's body is made from quartersawn white-oak scraps. The "rice paper" behind the slats is actually acrylic ($4 for an 18" x 24" sheet) that I sanded on both sides with a random-orbit sander and installed in the lantern using waterproof silicone.

The light fixture itself ($3 from my nearby home center) is vinyl clad and is intended for outdoor use. It's also installed in the base of the lamp using silicone.

Construction

There's no complicated joinery in this project, but it does require more precision and care than most outdoor furniture. Essentially, the four panels are glued at the edges to the four posts. This is a long-grain-to-long-grain joint, so no real joinery is required. However, to keep all the parts aligned during glue-up, I used a single No. 10 biscuit in each joint. This saved me some real headaches when clamping.

The lamp base, which holds the light fixture, rests on two cleats nailed to the inside of the panels. The removable top is held in position by four cleats nailed to the underside of the top.

Make sure you hold or clamp the stock firmly against your miter gauge's fence as you raise the dado stack. If you let the workpiece shift, it's very likely that it will self-destruct in your hands.

Clamp the post with one corner facing up. Check the grain direction and start planing. Begin with short strokes at the top of the post and, as your taper lengthens, make your strokes longer.

Taper

Begin construction by cutting out all your parts. Cutting the five ⅜"-wide slots in the panels – the first task – is the trickiest part of the whole project. Once you do that, you can breathe easier.

There are several ways to cut these slots. A plunge router with an edge guide is an obvious way to go about it. I chose to use a dado stack in my table saw. Place a dado stack measuring ⅜" wide into your table saw and get out your miter gauge or table saw sled, which will hold the work during the cut. You'll make a plunge cut into the panel for each slot.

First pencil a line on both long edges of the panel that shows where the slot should start and end. Position your panel slightly back of the blade's center, then raise the blade until it emerges from the panel and has nibbled to the far line. Move the piece forward until the dado stack nibbles to the near line. Lower the dado stack back under the saw's table, move the workpiece over ¾" and repeat the same process.

If you're feeling like these slots are more work then they're worth, consider other patterns. You can drill a series of holes with a drill press, or you can use a scroll saw to create a design that suits your brand of outdoor parties.

After all of your panels are cut, sand them to their finished grit or take a handplane to them before turning your attention to milling the four posts.

Five-sided Posts
As I mentioned earlier, I used a biscuit in each joint to line everything up during assembly. Now it's time to cut those biscuit slots. Mark the location of each slot and cut a recess for a No. 10 biscuit in each post and in each long edge of the panels.

You could leave the posts square and your lantern will look fine. I tapered one corner to give the lantern a lighter look. The taper clips ⅜" off the top outside corner of each post and then tapers to nothing at the base.

Some woodworkers might build a jig to make this cut. The simplest way is to mark the taper in pencil on the post, then plane down to that line using a block plane or bench plane. Each post should take less than five minutes to complete.

Sand your posts to their final grit and you're ready for assembly.

Assembly
Don't try to glue up all four posts at once. You'll want to be able to adjust the panels and posts as you clamp

Load your sander with #100-grit sandpaper and sand both sides of the acrylic. It takes only a couple of minutes to turn the clear plastic into frosted plastic.

everything, and eight parts sliding around is enough to make any woodworker panic.

When deciding which posts should go where, take a look at the figure. Each post should have one face that is flat-sawn grain and one that is quartersawn grain. Position the posts so the flat-sawn grain faces are together and the quartersawn grain faces are together. This is one of those things that might bug you about a project years later.

Begin by gluing up two assemblies that have two posts and one panel. While the glue is drying, nail the cleats for the lamp base to the other two panels in the location shown in the illustration at right. Then glue the two assemblies to the two remaining panels.

Final Details
Next, turn your attention to the top. Begin by cutting the ⅜" x ⅜" chamfer on the underside of all four edges. To let the heat from the light bulb escape, drill four ⅜"-diameter holes in the top, following the diagram.

Glue and nail the spacers to the top. Then add the top caps on top of the spacers. Screw and glue the feet centered on the posts.

The light fixture I purchased for this lantern was designed to sit in a 1½"-diameter hole. Drill the hole for your fixture in the center of the lamp base and attach the fixture to the base using silicone. Then attach the lamp base to the cleats using (again) a little dab of silicone.

The "rice paper" is my favorite part of the project. It's made from inexpensive ³⁄₃₂"-thick acrylic I bought at my local hardware store in the glass section. Cut the acrylic to size using your table saw and sand both faces with a random-orbit sander to get a frosted effect. Attach acrylic to the inside face of each panel using silicone. A spring clamp will hold it in place while the silicone cures.

Four cleats hold the top in position on the base. Turn the entire lamp upside down on your bench with the base centered on the underside of the top. Mark the location of the base. Measure in from those lines the combined thickness of the panels and the acrylic. Then nail four cleats at those locations.

As for the finish, I left mine natural for now. I might someday put a few coats of an outdoor finish on it, such as tung oil. But first I want to see if it survives our next outdoor party.

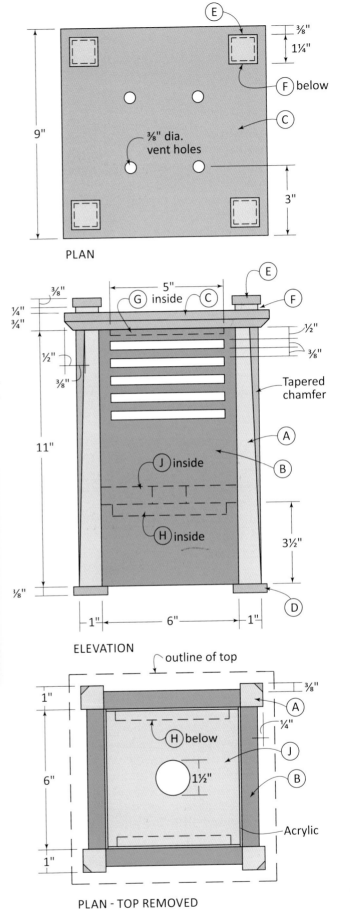

Outdoor Lantern

NO.	LET.	ITEM	DIMENSIONS (INCHES)		
			T	W	L
4	A	Posts	1	1	11
4	B	Panels	³⁄₄	6	11
1	C	Top	³⁄₄	9	9
4	D	Feet	³⁄₈	1½	1½
4	E	Top caps	³⁄₈	1¼	1¼
4	F	Spacers	¼	1	1
4	G	Cleats to hold top	¼	¼	5
2	H	Cleats to hold lamp base	½	½	5
1	J	Lamp base	³⁄₄	5⅞	5⅞

nineteen

Hand Mirrors

by ROBERT W. LANG

The way something looks is only the first half of a design problem. How to make it and how to make it efficiently are often greater challenges. If you want to make more than one of something, the problem grows exponentially. I designed these hand mirrors as a production item about 30 years ago. They are an example of making good choices from available options for quality and efficiency.

My goal was to appeal to the senses, both visual and tactile. Starting with nice wood helps on both counts. To get the handle right I made a few prototypes. I had to remember that not everybody has hands as big as mine. With the form established, I needed to duplicate the overall shape, with room to adapt each piece to the board it was cut from.

Most of the mirror is shaped by machine, but the handles are carved by hand. After a few runs of making these from a plywood pattern, I began to wish I could see through the pattern to better match the grain to the shape, and to more efficiently nest a batch of mirrors on a single board.

A trip to the local plastic fabricator's shop netted some ⅜"-thick Lexan. I traced the pattern on the sticky paper that covers the plastic, then cut the shape on the band saw. I smoothed out the saw marks on my disc and drum sanders, drilled a ³⁄₁₆"-diameter hole in the center, then removed the protective paper.

Feathering the Nest

It takes a piece of nice hardwood at least 6½" wide and 13¼" long to make one mirror. By reversing the pattern and arranging it handle to head, I can come close to doubling the yield when making several at a time. I put the pointy end of an awl in the hole in the pattern and tap the other end with a hammer.

That holds the pattern in place as I trace around it with a felt-tip marker. I can also rotate the pattern around the awl to adjust the way the grain of the wood follows the shape of the handle. At this point, it's tempting to head to the band saw to cut the blanks to shape, but it's better to put that off.

The mark left by the awl is the centerpoint of the circular cut out. I intended to make a router jig for the 5"-diameter holes, but that was too small to use a trammel on the router base to make the hole. I bought a fly cutter to make the pattern and a light came on while I was making the cut to make the pattern.

The fly cutter in the drill press is quicker and quieter than the router, even though it is a little on the scary side. I decided to use it to cut the holes, and here are a few tips to make it work well and safely. First and foremost is to clamp the work down to the drill press table. Second is to use the slowest possible speed on the drill press.

Inattention to either of these details can cause the drill press to perform an imitation of a crashing helicopter. It also helps to touch up the tip of the cutter with a file and sharpening stones. Repeat the sharpening if the cutter begins to burn or stall.

Stepped Rabbets

At this point, the front and back of the mirrors are the same. The difference in the finished product is that the back has a pair of offset rabbets. The first is ⅜" wide by the thickness of the back insert. The second one is ¼" wide and ⅛" deeper. The mirror fits in the deeper rabbet and is held in place by the insert.

Right-handed people generally prefer to hold a hand mirror in their left hand; so that from the front, the curve of the handle points to

Crystal clear. A transparent pattern, made from ⅜"-thick Lexan, makes it easy to adjust the position of the wood grain to the shape of the mirror.

the right. I mark which side will be the back, then cut the rabbets with a bearing-guided bit in a router. I set the depth to the material that will become the backs, nominally 5⁄16". Milling the rabbets before cutting the outside shapes gives the router a solid base to sit on, and plenty of room to clamp the work down.

I make a test cut on the edge of the board, then place a piece of the back material in the rabbet to make sure that the top surfaces are flush. When the first rabbets are done, change the setup to cut the second ones. Most rabbet bits can take different size bearings to cut different widths. Make sure that the second rabbet is deep enough to hold the mirror.

At some point after the rabbets are cut, schedule a break and head to your local glass shop. Take one of the blanks with you to be sure that the mirrors will fit. Glass people have trouble sometimes with esoteric technical terms like "perfect circle" and "5½" diameter."

Round & Round

The puzzle of how best to make the inserts perfectly round and exactly the right size took a while to solve. Woodworking books and magazines are full of nifty ways to make circles, but most of them didn't work well enough for me. Here are a few of the methods I tried, and the reasons I didn't like them.

Fly safely. A fly cutter works well for making large holes, but watch your hands. Clamp the work to the table securely and use the slowest possible speed.

Orderly steps. Mill the rabbets before cutting the blanks to shape. That leaves material to support the router, and to clamp the work to the bench.

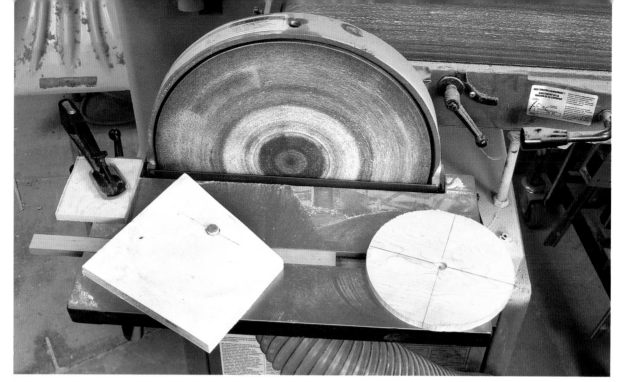

Swing it. The base of this jig pivots, allowing for adjustments to the diameter while in use. The short dowel registers in the hole centered in the back piece.

Stop on a dime.
A block of wood clamped to the table limits the size of the disc. Slide the jig away from the stop to take a deeper cut.

A jig for the band saw is hard to get started, leaves a rough edge and takes too long to dial in to the right size. A jig on the router table can leave a clean edge, but the small size puts hands too close to cutters, and there is a danger of tearing out a chunk of wood at some point on the curve. Turning the discs on the lathe makes for a smooth edge and you can sneak up on the exact size, but it takes too long in a production run to take the discs off and on the lathe to check the fit.

One of the surprises to me in making these mirrors was that there would always be some variation in the size and/or the shape of the holes. I wanted the thin discs to pop into the back without showing a gap, but they can't be too big and forced in without the risk of breaking the surrounding wood. I needed a magic device that would give me a perfect circle, and do it quickly. And I needed to get the wood on and off so

Rough shave. Hand work changes the curves from dull to varied, to improve the looks and the fit in the hand.

Rough to ready. A series of rasps removes the facets left by the spokeshave, eases the transitions between the curves and refines the shape.

Like magic. A card scraper is ideal for following the rasp. It slices off the ridges left by the teeth of the rasp, leaving a smooth surface.

that I could fit individual discs to individual holes, altering the shape slightly if I needed to.

I came up with a gizmo that works with a 12" disc sander. It's a piece of ½"-thick plywood with a ½"-diameter dowel that sticks up ⅛". A shallow hole is drilled with a Forstner bit in the back of each disc-to-be, so it can spin on the dowel. My moment of good thinking in this was to make the plywood plate pivot on a screw that connects the plate to a piece of wood that fits snugly in the miter gauge slot of the sander's table.

That allows the jig to pivot toward the disc, letting me reduce the diameter in controlled steps. It also allows me to clamp a stop on the table to limit the travel of the plate. I mark the discs with a compass on both faces of the material, taking care to align the centerpoints.

The compass point on the back side becomes the center for drilling the shallow hole, and the outline on the other side lets me know how close I am as I sand. I rough cut the discs on the band saw, staying as close as I can to the lines while moving at a productive pace. Then it's a stop at the drill press to make the holes before taking the stack to the sander.

At the sander, the early going can be aggressive, but I lighten up as the disc nears the pencil line. I make a test fit to see how much more material needs to be removed. I check the fit all the way around, because the shape of the hole may not be perfectly round due to some movement in the wood.

This happens across the grain, so wood has to be sanded from either both sides, or the top and bottom. As long as there is no obvious gap, no one will know it isn't a perfect circle. When I have a back fit to a blank, I leave it in place as much as possible during the remaining steps. This makes it easy to keep track of what goes where, and it keeps the holes from distorting if the wood decides to move.

Get a Handle On It

The overall length of the mirror leaves just enough room to cut all the way around on a 14" band saw. I make an initial rough cut to separate the blanks, then cut to the line. Then saw marks are removed with the disc and spindle sanders. It's important to make a smooth transition where the curve changes direction at the bottom of the radius.

After sanding, I go around the outer edge on both sides with a ⅜"-radius roundover bit at the router table. I mill the blanks as thick as possible from 4/4 stock, and make sure it is at least 1³⁄₁₆" thick. That leaves a flat area for the bearing of the router bit to ride against when routing the second side. I switch to a ¼"-radius bit to round over the inner circle on the face side.

Shaping the handles by hand is the step that makes these mirrors special, and for me it's the most enjoyable part of the process. The router removes much of the waste, and I use a spokeshave to increase the radius of the curves at the end of the handle, reduce the thick-

Stick with it. A thin bead of silicone adhesive holds both the mirror and the back in place. Keep the bead small to avoid squeeze-out.

ness directly below the mirror and blend the transitions between the machine-shaped and hand-shaped surfaces.

I use the spokeshave as a roughing tool, and skew the blade so that it takes a deep cut on one side and a more refined cut on the other. By shifting the tool laterally I control how much material is removed without changing tools or adjusting the tool. I work with the grain of the wood as I shape the handle. When it feels good and looks good, it's time to move on.

Avoiding the Fuss

There are many options to take a piece of wood from shaped-but-rough to ready-to-finish. This is a simple project, but some surfaces are flat, some have been rounded with a router, and some have been cut with a spokeshave. When the finish goes on, all of these surfaces need to be consistently smooth, and without a discernible transition from one shaping method to another.

My next move is to work on the transitions, and remove the facets left by the spokeshave. A rasp is ideal for this, even though the overall surface quality may look worse for a while. A coarse rasp with a round profile on one side will easily follow the curves, knocking off the high points. A finer rasp comes next, and its job is to remove the marks left in the wake of the coarse rasp.

A third rasp, with an even finer grain follows, to take out the marks left by its predecessor. The key to efficiency is knowing when to stop, when one tool has refined a surface as well as it can. If you start with too fine a tool (or too-fine sandpaper), you spend more time than you need to. The same thing happens if you keep going with a coarse tool, expecting it to leave a nicer surface than it can.

I follow the last rasp with a card scraper. Even the best rasp leaves behind a scratchy surface. The beauty of the scraper is that it only needs to knock off the high points the rasp left behind. It may seem like an unneeded complication to use these different tools, but each step is efficient and doesn't take long.

Some sanding is inevitable, but my goal is to make it as painless as possible. Refining the surfaces beforehand allows me to start with a relatively fine grit. For these mirrors, I start with a #120-grit piece of Abranet, backed up with a flexible pad. The pad makes it easy for the sandpaper to conform to the curves.

The first round of sanding is always the slowest, and if I come across an area that won't smooth quickly, I back up a step – to the scraper, a coarser grit of sandpaper or to the finest rasp. I repeat the sanding with a series of finer grits, working up to #240 or #280. As with the rasps, each step takes less time than the one before it.

I like the look and feel of an oil finish on small projects such as this, but oil can take weeks to achieve a decent build. I shortcut the process by applying one coat of Danish oil, rubbed in with a non-woven abrasive pad and then wiped dry. I let that sit overnight, then spray three or four coats of satin lacquer.

I allow the lacquer to dry thoroughly, then assemble the mirrors. I put the wood face down, then drop the round mirror into the recess. A narrow bead of silicone adhesive is applied to the outer edge of the mirror, then the back is put in position. Use a couple spring clamps to hold the back in place until the adhesive dries.

twenty

Heirloom Photo Album

by STEVE SHANESY

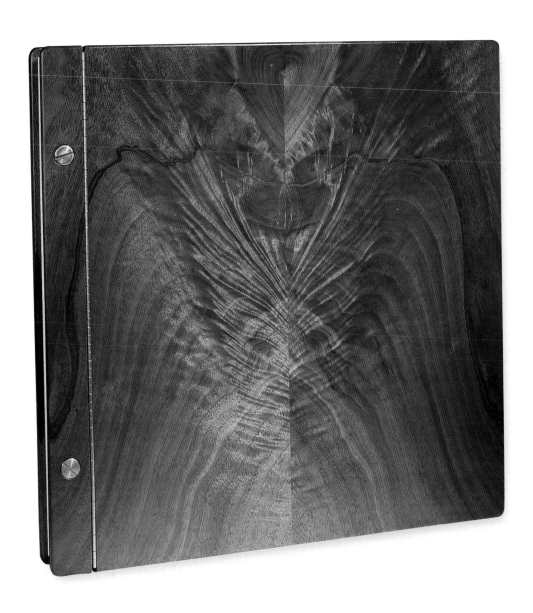

Why settle for an ordinary photo album when you can make your own?

Here is an easy and fun project. It could even be simpler than what you see here if you skip the resawing and bookmatching of the ¼"-thick front and back covers.

In fact, if you were making five or six at a time, you could probably spend no more than a half hour on each one. Or, you could go in the other direction and make it more complicated with inlay or chip carving on the front.

There could, in fact, be many variations on this project. You could easily alter the size of the covers for smaller photo album sheets, you could set it up with blank pages for use as a personal journal, or documents from your family tree research.

No matter what direction your version of this project takes, two simple elements will make it all possible: the post binding screws that fix the covers and pages together, and the small-scale continuous hinge that allows the covers to open, making them truly functional. The hinges and post binding screws can be ordered through the Lee Valley woodworking catalog.

Getting Started

A trip to an art or office-supply store is the first step. Select the photo page size you want to work with. Some pages simply are plain sheets that are inserted in clear plastic sheet protectors. The protectors, in turn, are usually punched for use in a three-ring binder. The sheets I used were hole punched for post binding and "hinged," meaning each sheet was made to fold at a given place along the edge where it would be bound into the album.

I selected a sheet size that was 12" x 12". Next I ordered my post binding screws and hinge from Lee Valley. The screws, called "Chicago Bolts" in the catalog, come in various lengths, with each length allowing for a ¼" adjustment. The brass hinge comes in a 3' length and is easily cut.

The page size and hinge gave me dimensions I could start to work with. The wood covers' finished size is ¼" x 12½" square. This allows ¼" for the cover to overlap top and bottom. The bound side has ⅛"overlap, leaving ⅜" for the open side. When I cut the pieces I made the width 12⅝". This allowed a table saw cut to separate the binding strip from the cover piece. The cover thickness was ¼", which is perfect for the hinge leaf.

A Word About Wood Choice

My album covers are made using feather-figured walnut that was resawn and bookmatched. It came from a tree in my neighborhood that was taken down and sawn into lumber about three years ago. Although it's been air drying all this time I was nervous as a cat about my pieces warping after resawing and glue up. Highly figured wood often has a mind of its own. I know that walnut is a relatively stable wood, like mahogany, but I kept my pieces on a flat surface with a weight on top until I was able to put a finish on them. Even at the thin ¼" dimension, I was lucky and both pieces have remained perfectly flat.

The point of all this is to remind you to be cautious about your wood selection and handling. Try to use a stable species. A narrower album would be less risky.

Hardware Installation & Finishing

I followed the hole patterns for the post binding screws that were already in the album sheets. Allowing for the top and bottom overhang, my hole center for the screws was 2⁹⁄₁₆" from the top and bottom. From the binding edge, I marked a hole center of ½".

The posts required a ¼" hole with a ½"-diameter counterbore to recess the flat heads of the screws. I used a Forstner bit for drilling in my drill press. It is necessary to drill the front and back banding strip exactly alike.

At this point I progressively sanded to #220-grit, rounded the outside corners to a ³⁄₁₆" radius, and heavily eased the edges, except for the edges where the hinge would be installed.

The finish may be a bit more complicated than you are accustomed to, but the fantastic figure in the walnut demanded as good a finish as I know how. And it was worth each step. Because walnut is an open-pore wood, I filled the grain using paste wood filler. I added oil-based walnut stain to the filler to color the filler and the wood. After applying the filler, I allowed it to dry for 24 hours.

For a clear top coat I used a lacquer that comes in an aerosol spray can. The product is the best lacquer in a can I've ever used. It's called Master's Magic and is available from The Woodturners Catalog. A can of sanding sealer and satin finish lacquer are required, and the product should be used only in a well-ventilated area free of open flames (including pilot lights on water heaters or furnaces) or potential sparks.

After applying the sanding sealer, carefully sand with #360-grit paper, being especially careful near the

supplies

Lee Valley Tools
leevalley.com or 800-871-8158

Brass piano hinge,
12mm x 800mm,
#00D50.12, $7.40

Brass escutcheon pins,
flat head, #00D41.02 $2.60

Chicago bolts, brass,
30 - 36mm, 4 pack,
#00K40.05, $4.70

Craft Supplies USA
woodturnerscatalog.com
800-551-8876

Masters Magic Lacquer Sanding Sealer,
aerosol can, #299-0100, $10.95

Masters Magic Satin Spray Lacquer,
aerosol can,
#299-0001, $10.95

Prices correct at time of publication.

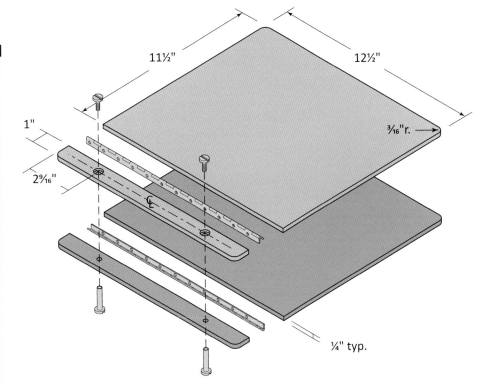

EXPLODED VIEW

Brass miniature continuous hinges are a cinch to cut with a pair of metal shears. Make your cut at the joint where two hinge leaves meet nearest your ideal length.

An ordinary paper hole punch enlarged the holes that were pre-punched by the manufacturer of the photo album sheets.

edges. The idea is to lightly sand down any dust particles or bubbles that may have formed but not to sand into the stain color below the sealer. After sanding the sealer, spray two top coats with the satin finish. Allow the finish to cure overnight, even though it will be dry to the touch in 15 minutes.

I used a pair of snips to cut the hinges to 12⅛" long. Cut the hinge at one of the leaf joints. The hinges are attached using flat-head brads that you should order along with the hinges. Predrill the holes for the brads into the edge of the wood leaving about ¼" of the brad length not drilled. Predrilling should ensure nothing pokes though the face of the cover.

Insert the post part of the post binding screws and fill your photo page inserts. I found that it was necessary to slightly enlarge the holes in the sheets with an ordinary paper punch. When done, lay the other cover over the post and then insert the screw.

If you are considering leaving the album on a coffee tabletop, or if you just want to protect the back cover from scratches, put a felt bumper pad in each corner of the back cover.

As a photo album or scrap book, this project makes an extra special gift for an extra special occasion. Is there a family wedding in your future?

contributors

ANDY BROWNELL
Andy has studied woodworking extensively with Jeff Miller since 1996. A full-time ad man, Andy still finds time to build custom furniture in his Cincinnati-area workshop.

MEGAN FITZPATRICK
Megan is the editor of *Popular Woodworking Magazine*.

GLEN D. HUEY
Glen is a former senior editor with *Popular Woodworking Magazine* and the author of several woodworking books.

JOSHUA KLEIN
Joshua is a furniture conservator and period furniture maker who lives and works in Brooklin, Maine.

ROBERT W. LANG
Robert is a former senior editor with *Popular Woodworking Magazine* and the author of several woodworking books.

RANEY NELSON
Raney is an infill planemaker and woodworker at Daed Toolworks (daedtoolworks.com); his shop is located near Indianapolis, Ind.

CHRISTOPHER SCHWARZ
Chris is a former editor of *Popular Woodworking Magazine* (now contributing editor) and is the editor at Lost Art Press.

TROY SEXTON
Troy Sexton designs and builds custom furniture in Sunbury, Ohio, for his company, Sexton Classic American Furniture. Troy is a contributing editor for Popular Woodworking.

STEVE SHANESY
Steve is a former editor and publisher of *Popular Woodworking Magazine* and Popular Woodworking Books.

DAVID THIEL
David Thiel is a former senior editor for *Popular Woodworking Magazine* and now creates videos for the Popular Woodworking brand.

JOHN WILSON
John has been teaching people how to make Shaker oval boxes for more than 30 years. He teaches the traditional craft across the country. Besides teaching and selling his boxes, John founded The Home Shop to produce supplies for oval box makers worldwide.

Simple & Stylish Woodworking. Copyright © 2017 by Popular Woodworking Books. Printed and bound in China. All rights reserved. No part of this book may be reproduced in any form or by any electronic or mechanical means including information storage and retrieval systems without permission in writing from the publisher, except by a reviewer, who may quote brief passages in a review. Published by Popular Woodworking Books, an imprint of F+W Media, Inc., 10151 Carver Rd. Blue Ash, Ohio, 45242. First edition.

Distributed in Canada by Fraser Direct
100 Armstrong Avenue
Georgetown, Ontario L7G 5S4
Canada

Distributed in the U.K. and Europe by
F&W Media International
Pynes Hill Court
Pynes Hill
Rydon Lane
Exeter
EX2 5AZ
United Kingdom
Tel: (+44) 1392 797680

Visit our website at popularwoodworking.com or our consumer website at shopwoodworking.com for more woodworking information.

Other fine Popular Woodworking Books are available from your local bookstore or direct from the publisher.

ISBN-13: 978-1-4403-5167-9

21   20   19   18   17   5   4   3   2   1

Editor: *Scott Francis*
Cover Designer: *Daniel T. Pessell*
Interior Designer: *Angela Lennert Wilcox*
Production Coordinator: *Debbie Thomas*

Read This Important Safety Notice

To prevent accidents, keep safety in mind while you work. Use the safety guards installed on power equipment. When working on power equipment, keep fingers away from saw blades, wear safety goggles to prevent injuries from flying wood chips and sawdust, wear hearing protection and consider installing a dust vacuum to reduce the amount of airborne sawdust in your woodshop. Don't wear loose clothing or jewelry when working on power equipment. Tie back long hair to prevent it from getting caught in your equipment. People who are sensitive to certain chemicals should check the chemical content of any product before using it. The authors and editors who compiled this book have tried to make the contents as accurate and correct as possible. Plans, illustrations, photographs and text have been carefully checked. All instructions, plans and projects should be carefully read, studied and understood before beginning construction. Due to the variability of local conditions, construction materials, skill levels, etc., neither the author nor Popular Woodworking Books assumes any responsibility for any accidents, injuries, damages or other losses incurred resulting from the material presented in this book. Prices listed for supplies and equipment were current at the time of publication and are subject to change.

METRIC CONVERSION CHART

To convert	to	multiply by
Inches	Centimeters	2.54
Centimeters	Inches	0.4
Feet	Centimeters	30.5
Centimeters	Feet	0.03
Yards	Meters	0.9
Meters	Yards	1.1

a content + ecommerce company

Ideas ▪ Instruction ▪ Inspiration

Receive FREE downloadable bonus materials when you sign up for our FREE newsletter at **popularwoodworking.com**.

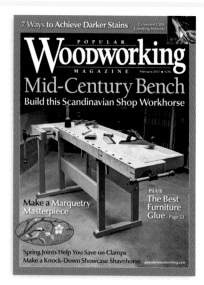

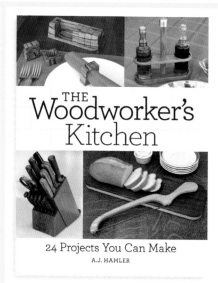

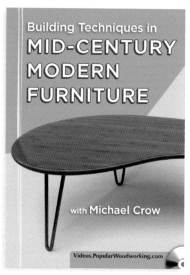

Find the latest issues of *Popular Woodworking* Magazine on newsstands, or visit **popularwoodworking.com**.

These and other great Popular Woodworking products are available at your local bookstore, woodworking store or online supplier. Visit our website at **shopwoodworking.com**.

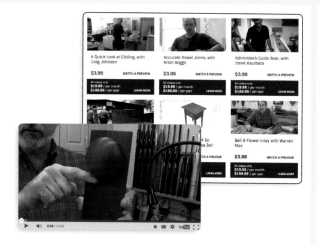

Popular Woodworking Videos

Subscribe and get immediate access to the web's best woodworking subscription site. You'll find more than 400 hours of woodworking video tutorials and full-length video workshops from world-class instructors on workshops, projects, SketchUp, tools, techniques and more! **videos.popularwoodworking.com**

Visit our Website

Find helpful and inspiring articles, videos, blogs, projects and plans at **popularwoodworking.com**.

 For behind the scenes information, become a fan at **Facebook.com/popularwoodworking**.

 For more tips, clips and articles, follow us at **twitter.com/pweditors**.

 For visual inspiration, follow us at **pinterest.com/popwoodworking**.

 For free videos visit **youtube.com/popwoodworking**.

 Follow us on Instagram **@popwoodworking**.